T0286807

Cambridge Elements ≡

Elements in the Problems of God
edited by
Michael L. Peterson
Asbury Theological Seminary

GOD AND THE PROBLEM OF EVIDENTIAL AMBIGUITY

Max Baker-Hytch
University of Oxford

CAMBRIDGE
UNIVERSITY PRESS

Shaftesbury Road, Cambridge CB2 8EA, United Kingdom

One Liberty Plaza, 20th Floor, New York, NY 10006, USA

477 Williamstown Road, Port Melbourne, VIC 3207, Australia

314–321, 3rd Floor, Plot 3, Splendor Forum, Jasola District Centre,
New Delhi – 110025, India

103 Penang Road, #05–06/07, Visioncrest Commercial, Singapore 238467

Cambridge University Press is part of Cambridge University Press & Assessment,
a department of the University of Cambridge.

We share the University's mission to contribute to society through the pursuit of
education, learning and research at the highest international levels of excellence.

www.cambridge.org
Information on this title: www.cambridge.org/9781009462341

DOI: 10.1017/9781009269841

When citing this work, please include a reference to the DOI 10.1017/9781009269841

First published 2023

A catalogue record for this publication is available from the British Library.

ISBN 978-1-009-46234-1 Hardback
ISBN 978-1-009-26987-2 Paperback
ISSN 2754-8724 (online)
ISSN 2754-8716 (print)

God and the Problem of Evidential Ambiguity

Elements in the Problems of God

DOI: 10.1017/9781009269841
First published online: December 2023

Max Baker-Hytch
University of Oxford

Author for correspondence: Max Baker-Hytch, max.baker-hytch@wycliffe
.ox.ac.uk

Abstract. When it comes to what many of us think of as the deepest
questions of existence, the answers can seem difficult to make out. This
difficulty, or ambiguity, is the topic of this Element. The Element begins
by offering a general account of what evidential ambiguity consists in
and uses it to try to make sense of the idea that our world is religiously
ambiguous in some sense. It goes on to consider the questions of how
we ought to investigate the nature of ultimate reality and whether
evidential ambiguity is itself a significant piece of evidence in the quest.

This Element also has a video abstract: www.cambridge.org/baker-hytch

Keywords: ambiguity, evidence, God, worldview, investigation

ISBNs: 9781009462341 (HB), 9781009269872 (PB), 9781009269841 (OC)
ISSNs: 2754-8724 (online), 2754-8716 (print)

Contents

1 What Is the Problem of Evidential Ambiguity?

Something that is ambiguous is difficult to make out. Difficult, but perhaps not impossible. When it comes to what many of us think of as the deepest questions of existence, the answers can seem difficult to make out. Difficult, but perhaps not impossible. The difficulty that we seem to have in figuring out what reality is all about, the ambiguity that seems to confront us when we ponder the deep questions of existence, is the topic of this Element.

Evidential ambiguity is the term I shall use to refer to difficulty in working out whether a particular proposition is true or false, given a particular set of evidence. When it comes to propositions concerning the nature of ultimate reality, in what does the difficulty consist? Is it something about the way the world is, or something about us, or some combination of the two that gives rise to a sense of ambiguity? Given this situation that we find ourselves in, what might be the best way to try to investigate questions concerning whether there's a God, an afterlife, whether the mind is just the brain, and so on? And might the existence of ambiguity *itself* be a piece of evidence that points in a particular direction? The importance of questions like these is obvious to most people, regardless of whether someone has formally studied philosophy. And whilst there has undoubtedly been considerable philosophical work done on some aspects of these issues, these questions seem to me to form an interrelated cluster or family of epistemological issues that are worthy of being addressed as a single topic, to which I suggest we give the name *the problem of evidential ambiguity*. The aim of this Element, then, is to begin to map out the contours of the problem of evidential ambiguity and to suggest possible avenues that we might pursue in seeking to gain a better grasp of it.

1.1 Ultimate Reality and Worldview

Before we go any further, it is important for us to get clearer on a pair of terms that will be used frequently throughout this Element, namely *ultimate reality* and *worldview*. Robert Nozick offers a particularly helpful discussion of what might be meant by the former term. He writes that

> The notion of ultimate reality can refer to different things ... : the ground-floor stuff out of which everything is composed; the fundamental explanatory level which explains all current happenings; the factor out of which every-thing else originated; the goal toward which everything develops ... These different modes of ultimacy do share a common feature, though. Ultimacy always marks the extreme end of an ordering. This ordering can be based upon a chain of explanation, a chain of origination, a chain of further and further goals, etc. In each case, what is ultimate comes at the extreme end of

> an ordering, an important and extremely lengthy, perhaps even infinite,
> ordering – its position there is what makes it ultimate. (1989: 200)

J. L. Schellenberg (2016: 168) helpfully labels the four kinds of ultimacy highlighted in the first sentence of the passage just quoted as follows: (1) *compositional* ultimacy ('the ground-floor stuff out of which everything is composed'); (2) *explanatory* ultimacy ('the fundamental explanatory level which explains all current happenings'); (3) *generative* ultimacy ('the factor out of which everything else originated'); (4) *teleological* ultimacy ('the goal toward which everything develops').

The foregoing list isn't exhaustive of all the kinds of ultimacy that there could be, however. Schellenberg himself discusses three kinds of ultimacy: metaphysical, axiological, and soteriological. Metaphysical ultimacy is close to Nozick's explanatory ultimacy. But the other two kinds seem not to be equivalent to anything in Nozick's list. Thus we have (5) *axiological* ultimacy, which is a matter of something's being 'ultimate in inherent value – the greatest possible reality' (Schellenberg, 2016: 169), and (6) *soteriological* ultimacy, which is a matter of something's being (or, perhaps, being the source of) the greatest good that is attainable in the lives of creatures. Following Nozick and Schellenberg, then, I suggest that the term 'ultimate reality' is polyvalent but that its various meanings are nevertheless interrelated.

As the field of philosophy of religion has begun to broaden beyond just discussing theism and naturalism, it has become useful to have a term that refers to any suitably comprehensive system of claims about the nature of ultimate reality, and the term 'worldview' has seemed to various contemporary authors to fit the bill (e.g., Oppy, 2017). A worldview is a theory about what is ultimate in any of the senses just outlined. A worldview can, of course, be much more than a theory, but for something to count as a worldview it does have to be *at least* a theory, one which has certain aspirations in terms of explanatory scope and depth. I would hesitate to suggest that to count as a worldview a theory must offer answers to the question of what is ultimate in all six aforementioned senses, but a worldview will typically have something to say about most of these various forms of ultimacy – even if the answer it offers is that *nothing* is ultimate in a given sense. It is worth noting that most of the major worldviews offer answers to the question of the postmortem fate of human beings and the relationship between the mind and the body. Rather than see these as additional facets beyond the six forms of ultimacy outlined, I would suggest that such claims can be seen to comprise answers to the questions of what is ultimate in senses (1) and (4).

A worldview need not be religious, hence why the term *worldview* is useful for discussing a wide variety of views about the nature of ultimate reality. There have been innumerable attempts to specify what makes some worldviews religious and others non-religious. Whilst I don't have space to enter into that particular discussion here, I would note a particularly compelling recent proposal from Sam Lebens (2022). According to Lebens, a worldview is religious just in case it calls for *religiosity*, where that involves (i) the fostering of a community built around shared commitments; (ii) the having of propositional faith in some key claims about the nature of ultimate reality; and (iii) participation in practices that draw the practitioner into an imaginative engagement with some of these claims.

There are, of course, innumerable worldviews on offer in the present day, but it can be helpful to group them into families. A fairly natural way of grouping them is into the following three families: theistic worldviews, naturalistic worldviews, and impersonal non-naturalistic worldviews.

Theistic worldviews are those worldviews that have at their core the claim that the fundamental explanation of the world we observe is an uncreated personal being to whom the title 'God' (or a non-English equivalent term) is usually given, and who possesses very large or unlimited degrees of great-making properties such as power, knowledge, goodness, and so on. More specific versions of theism claim that God has additional attributes over and above those just mentioned and also that specific events or persons in human history are vehicles of revelation concerning the nature and purposes of God. Theistic worldviews typically, though not invariably, claim that the goal of human life is union with God, and that some kind of conscious existence awaits us beyond the grave.

Naturalistic worldviews are those that have at their core the claim that that which is most fundamental explanatorily is both impersonal and physical, in the sense that it consists entirely of the sorts of substances and properties that could in principle feature in a scientific account of the world. According to such worldviews, consciousness is either generated out of wholly physical substances and properties or is simply identical with wholly physical substances and properties. Naturalistic worldviews typically hold that there are no purposes inherent in the universe, although human beings are perhaps free to generate purposes of their own, and that conscious experience ceases permanently at death.

Impersonal non-naturalistic worldviews are those that have at their core the claim that that which is most fundamental explanatorily is impersonal and yet is neither identical to nor is generated by physical entities. Some, though not by any means all, forms of pantheism belong in this grouping. Some forms of pantheism are metaphysically naturalistic in that they claim that God is simply identical with the physical universe – probably Baruch Spinoza's pantheism was of this kind (see Leftow, 2016: 64–5). Other forms of pantheism, however, do seem to claim that the fundamental explanatory layer of reality is non-physical. An example of this might be the Advaita Vedānta tradition of Indian philosophy (see Dalal, 2021), which claims, very roughly, that ultimate reality is an impersonal absolute consciousness that underlies finite consciousnesses and will eventually reabsorb them all. Other worldviews that belong in this category might include John Leslie's axiarchism (2016), on which an impersonal ultimate goodness is in some sense responsible for generating physical reality, and Schellenberg's ultimism (2016), according to which there is some impersonal but non-physical X, which is ultimate axiologically, metaphysically, and soteriologically.

I don't claim that these three groupings are exhaustive of all the possible worldviews that there could be, but they do account for the vast majority of worldviews actually held by human beings. Nor am I claiming to have identified necessary and sufficient conditions for a worldview to belong to one or other category. Rather, the preceding groupings reflect a family resemblance approach in which we note features that are typically (if not strictly necessarily) found among the members of a given family.

What of polytheism? The empirical evidence suggests that the majority of what are typically viewed as polytheistic worldviews are not such a far cry from monotheism, in that they often involve belief in a 'high god' who is the supreme creator of all else, including all other deities (Braddock, 2023). Some polytheistic worldviews, however, may turn out on close inspection to be forms of impersonal non-naturalism if what they claim is that all deities are dependent for their existence on some explanatorily more fundamental principle or force that is non-physical but impersonal.

A final word of clarification is needed before we go further. Throughout the Element I will speak of 'the question concerning the nature of ultimate reality' or equivalently of 'the worldview question'. What I mean by these phrases is the question of *which* set of claims about the nature of ultimate reality – which worldview – is true. I acknowledged that the three families of worldviews I just outlined do not exhaust all of the logically possible options. It is of course logically possible that none of the worldviews actually believed by humans is true. For that reason, I mean for the question of which worldview is true to be understood as ranging over all the logically possible worldviews, which is to say, all the logically coherent sets of statements about what is ultimate in the various senses outlined previously, including all those that no human being has ever thought of.

1.2 A Cluster of Problems

The issues that I wish to broach in this Element are undoubtedly related to the problem of divine hiddenness in contemporary philosophy of religion. The problem of divine hiddenness as it has been developed by J. L. Schellenberg (1993, 2007, 2015) is fundamentally a problem of violated expectations in relation to theistic worldviews. That is, it appears plausible to suppose that there are some human beings in our world who find themselves doubting the existence of God through no fault of their own – non-resistant non-believers, as they are termed in the literature – and this situation is not what one would expect to find if a perfectly loving God exists, or so the argument goes.

The hiddenness problem is a fascinating topic and one that has attracted a large amount of attention in the philosophy of religion literature over the past three decades. Much of it has taken the form of investigating whether there might be good reasons for a perfectly loving God to permit some people to be in a state of non-resistant non-belief for a time, or in other words, to permit there to be evidential ambiguity with regards to the existence of God (see, e.g., Howard-Snyder & Moser, 2002; Stump & Green, 2015; Weidner, 2021).

Divine hiddenness, then, is a problem for theism specifically. In this Element, however, my aim is to attempt to chart some of the less well-explored ways in which issues of evidential ambiguity might bear upon worldviews of all kinds, not just theistic ones. Many deeply committed adherents of a variety of worldviews acknowledge that the truth of their favoured worldview is not just overwhelmingly obvious, even though they will usually think that their worldview is reasonable on the overall balance of the evidence. Theist philosopher T. J. Mawson, for example, notes that whilst he takes various philosophical arguments for theism to have some real force, he considers that 'It's not that atheists are simply missing something obvious' (2013: 25). On the other side of the aisle, as it were, Graham Oppy thinks that there is a good cumulative case for the truth of naturalism and yet he writes that, 'I am also pretty firmly of the belief that, even by quite strict standards, those who believe in the existence of orthodoxly conceived monotheistic gods need not thereby manifest some kind of failure of rationality' (2006: xviii–xix). Statements like these are an implicit acknowledgement of the existence of some degree of ambiguity in the evidence concerning the nature of ultimate reality. Many more such statements from adherents of a variety of worldviews could be cited at this point.

All of this raises what I take to be an interesting cluster of questions:

(a) How exactly should we characterise this sense many people have (including many serious and committed adherents of a variety of worldviews who think that their worldview is reasonable on the total evidence) that the nature of ultimate reality is not completely obvious to us, or at any rate, that grasping it is not totally straightforward?

(b) Just *how* evidentially ambiguous is our situation as regards the nature of ultimate reality? And is there some way to characterise this that is world-view-neutral (in the sense that the characterisation we offer doesn't pre-suppose or privilege any particular worldview or family of worldviews)?

(c) How ought someone to go about investigating the nature of ultimate reality, given the difficulties that exist in working out how much weight to accord various kinds of evidence?

(d) To what extent is the phenomenon of evidential ambiguity itself evidence for or against various worldviews? Or, put another way, to what extent is evidential ambiguity to be expected conditional upon various different worldviews?

These are the questions that the remainder of this Element will seek to address. The remaining four sections will consider each of the four questions in turn.

Section 2 contends that the best way to make sense of the commonly voiced idea that the universe we inhabit is in some way ambiguous as regards the worldview question is to suppose that there is an important shared frame of reference, which I term *the public evidence*, that is comprised of the body of facts that are in principle knowable by way of non-inferential cognitive abilities that virtually all humans would recognise as real, and that it is relative to this body of truths that it is less than wholly obvious which worldview is true. I go on to offer a general account of what gives rise to evidential ambiguity in terms of the interrelation of three factors: one's cognitive abilities; one's vantage point; and the facts of the matter in question, including the sorts of traces and indicators that are generated by those facts.

Section 3 turns to the question of what exactly it could mean to describe that body of publicly accessible facts – the public evidence – as being evidentially ambiguous with respect to the worldview question. There are a number of accounts on offer in the contemporary philosophy of religion literature. I survey five such accounts, with a view to finding a way of characterising the evidential ambiguity of the public evidence that doesn't presuppose or privilege any particular worldview (or family of worldviews) and is genuinely interest-ing, which is to say, it is a characterisation that doesn't also apply to a large swathe of our other beliefs.

Section 4 takes on the question of how we ought to go about investigating the nature of ultimate reality, and compares two families of views on the issue, namely, *involved* and *detached* approaches, as I term them. The former approach counsels us to step inside a particular worldview and inhabit its way of life and thereby allegedly open ourselves to gaining insights that would otherwise be inaccessible. The question of how to decide *which* worldview to step inside is an enduring challenge for such an approach. The latter approach strives to utilise a quasi-scientific methodology for assembling the total relevant evidence and trying to ascertain its overall significance in as impartial a manner as possible. The biggest question for this kind of approach is whether the attempt to take stock of all the many bits of evidence and add them all up can really avoid being coloured by prior commitments and emotionally infused judgements. I propose an approach that is something of a hybrid of these two approaches.

Section 5 considers the way in which a situation that is evidentially ambiguous can itself be evidence for or against certain hypotheses, to the degree that an evidentially ambiguous situation is more what we would expect to find on some hypotheses than on others. An interesting question, then, is whether the evidential ambiguity pertaining to the worldview question is itself evidence that supports some worldviews over others. I explain how we should try to isolate the evidential contribution that evidential ambiguity itself makes from the contribution made by all the usual evidences that are standardly cited for and against various worldviews (fine-tuning, consciousness, reports of religious experiences, evil and suffering, and so on), and I offer some reasons for doubting that evidential ambiguity itself makes a substantial evidential contribution in its own right to the worldview question.

2 The Nature and Sources of Evidential Ambiguity

This section begins to address the question of what it might mean for a situation to be evidentially ambiguous and what are the factors in general that give rise to evidential ambiguity, thus paving the way for us to consider what it might mean to say that the nature of ultimate reality is evidentially ambiguous in some important sense.

2.1 Two Conceptions of Evidence

Before we go further, we need to say a bit about the concept of evidence, or indeed, the *concepts* of evidence – it is arguable that we employ more than one in everyday discourse. In a careful survey of the philosophical literature on the nature of evidence, Thomas Kelly notes that

> Of course, 'evidence' is hardly a philosopher's term of art: it is not only, or even primarily, philosophers who routinely speak of evidence, but also lawyers and judges, historians and scientists, investigative journalists and reporters, as well as the members of numerous other professions and ordinary

> folk in the course of everyday life. The concept of evidence would thus seem
> to be on firmer pre-theoretical ground than various other concepts which
> enjoy similarly central standing within philosophy. (2014)

Given the prominence of the term 'evidence' in ordinary discourse, it makes
sense to begin by reflecting on everyday usage of that term. Consider the
following utterances:

> Your evidence at the time of the incident made it reasonable to fear that there
> was a plot to oust you.
>   The committee's evidence was too finely balanced to enable them to reach
> a 'guilty' verdict in regard to the complaint that had been raised.

These statements, which I take it are perfectly well-formed English sentences,
seem to involve a notion of evidence as consisting in the information that is
within someone's purview at a given moment and as the determinant of the
degree to which a particular belief that that person holds is reasonable at that
moment. Evidence in this sense is something that is possessed by someone.
Kelly (2014) characterises evidence in this sense as 'that which justifies belief'
and suggests that it is synonymous with 'reason to believe'.

Contrast all of this with the way that the term 'evidence' is being used in the
following utterances:

> The police forensics team are examining the bungalow inch by inch in search
> of evidence of third-party involvement in the deaths.
>   These new radio telescopes have been set up to scan the night sky for
> possible evidence of extra-terrestrial intelligence.

These statements, which I take it are also perfectly well-formed English sentences, seem to involve a quite different notion of evidence. On this notion, it
seems that evidence consists of facts or objects that are 'out there' in the world
and that can in principle fall outside the purview of any agent. Kelly (2014)
discusses evidence in this sense as being 'a sign, symptom, or mark' of the thing
for which it is evidence.

In this section I am going to suggest that evidential ambiguity is a matter
of the relationship between the information that falls within a given person's purview (i.e., evidence in the first sense just discussed) and the facts
out there in the world that are a sign or indicator of the truth concerning
the topic in question (i.e., evidence in the second sense). The manner in
which the former overlaps with the latter is what determines the extent to
which a given question or topic is evidentially ambiguous, or so I shall
suggest.

2.2 Ambiguity as a Property of the World Itself?

Could it make any sense to ascribe the property of being evidentially ambiguous to *the world itself*? As we are about to see, several philosophers of religion have written in a way that makes it sound rather like they think so. One such philosopher was J. L. Schellenberg. At one point in his book *The Hiddenness Argument*, Schellenberg reminisces about how at an early point in his career he had initially thought that divine hiddenness should be characterised in terms of some mind-independent facts about the world – facts having to do with the overall balance of the evidence for and against the existence of God – but that he ended up thinking that the divine hiddenness problem was better framed simply in terms of facts about the failure of some humans (apparently blamelessly) to end up believing that God exists:

> By now I was at Oxford working toward the DPhil in philosophy. And there I realised that I had grabbed hold of the wrong end of the stick. The important thing to take away from the notion of religious ambiguity was not some sophisticated fact or facts about evidence out there in the world articulable by means of probability theory, in which my thesis supervisor, Richard Swinburne, was an expert, but rather simple facts about subjective states of people, such as that honest doubt about God is possible. (2015: 37)

Perhaps Schellenberg is correct that an argument from divine hiddenness can get off the ground just using claims about the states of human minds and can happily ignore questions about the state of the evidence 'out there in the world' (though Jonathan Kvanvig (2002) has argued that the hiddenness argument *does* crucially rely on a claim about the balance of the evidence for and against theism). But ordinarily when we observe that humans have divergent intellectual attitudes towards a particular subject matter, we are prompted to investigate whether there might be something about either the relevant human cognitive abilities or the subject matter itself which can account for the divergent responses.

A number of other authors in the field seem to harbour the same intuition that Schellenberg had initially pursued. Various philosophers of religion, including some theists and some non-theists, have written in a way that suggests that the world itself in some sense exhibits the property of being evidentially ambiguous (emphases in the following quotes are all mine):

> *Ronald Hepburn* (1963: 50): For how could *such an ambiguous universe* be the work of perfect love and perfect power?

> *Terence Penelhum* (1971: 214): Belief presents itself to the serious and concerned inquirer as a possible explanation of the world in which he finds

himself and a possible response to it ... Yet *the world does not point to its truth unambiguously.*

John Hick (1989: 73): By *the religious ambiguity of the universe* I do not mean that it has no definite character but that it is capable from our present human vantage point of being thought and experienced in both religious and naturalistic ways.

Robert McKim (2001: 22): *The world manifests ambiguity* in that it is open both to secular and to religious readings, but also in that it is open to a number of religious readings.

John Cottingham (2005: 112–13): *[T]he natural world itself* necessarily remains, from a certain perspective, *ambiguous, blank, poker-faced*; however well scrutinised, the intimations of a reality beyond or behind it will never be experienced unless the heart is open and receptive.

These expressions are interesting and, coming as they do from thinkers who hold a variety of views on the nature of ultimate reality, they are worth pondering. The challenge, however, is that it isn't easy to make sense of the idea that *the world itself*, independently of our perspectives on it, could be either ambiguous or unambiguous. Presumably if we had unlimited cognitive access to reality – that is, if we were omniscient – then we would encounter no ambiguity of any sort. Reality is perfectly consistent with itself and if we could apprehend every aspect of it we would presumably be left in no doubt as to its fundamental nature. To be fair, there are hints of further nuancing within some of the preceding quotations. Hick frames his statement with reference to 'our present human vantage point', and Cottingham's statement includes the words 'from a certain perspective', both of which may suggest that the ambiguity at issue is at least partly due to the limitations of our access to reality. Penelhum focuses on how the world 'points to' things, where perhaps implicitly it is to us humans that it is pointing things out. And McKim makes mention of multiple 'readings' of reality, which may suggest that ambiguity has something to do with the cognitive abilities of those doing the reading.

Approaching things as charitably as possible, I suggest that what the authors previously quoted may be trying to get at in their various ways is this: there is an important shared frame of reference relative to which the nature of ultimate reality is less than wholly obvious (what exactly is meant by its being 'less than wholly obvious' is the topic of Section 3). What I want to do now is to try to offer an account of what that shared frame of reference consists of; that is, I want to try to offer an account of what it is that might plausibly be thought to exhibit the property of being evidentially ambiguous. For the sake of ease, it will help if we can alight on a term for that shared frame of reference. I will use the term *the public evidence*.

2.3 The Public Evidence: A Shared Frame of Reference

As is already implicit in my preceding remarks, I think it makes little sense to identify the public evidence with the set of all truths (and in any case, there are set-theoretic worries about whether there can even be such a thing as a set of all truths). We cannot sensibly attribute the property of evidential ambiguity to the set of all truths, because the set of all truths of course includes the truth about which worldview is correct. The set of all truths includes the truth about whether God exists, about whether there is an afterlife, about what things of all kinds are composed of, about what (if anything) has ultimate value, and so on. In short, the set of all truths isn't even slightly ambiguous with respect to the nature of ultimate reality – or indeed, as regards any question at all.

A related option is to identify the public evidence with the set of all truths *except for* the truth about which worldview is correct. An immediate problem arises with this. Just suppose for the sake of argument that it is true that God spoke to Moses through a burning bush. The proposition that *God spoke to Moses through a burning bush* logically entails that there is a God; it entails that theism is true. A set of truths that includes *God spoke to Moses through a burning bush* can hardly be thought to be ambiguous with respect to the worldview question. So, it looks as though the public evidence – in order to be able to be meaningfully characterised as ambiguous – needs to exclude not only the truth about which worldview is correct, but additionally, all truths that logically entail the truth about which worldview is correct. The problem that now arises is that, where W is a true proposition stating which worldview is correct, and w is any true proposition that entails W, the exclusion of all truths w from the public evidence will effectively mean discounting any sound deductive arguments that may exist in support of a given worldview. While it is true that discussions over which worldview is true are increasingly being framed probabilistically and abductively, to have to exclude all deductive arguments from our investigations seems like a rather undesirable result, given the way that deductive arguments have been so much at the heart of philosophical debates about the nature of ultimate reality down the centuries.

Neither of the options just considered for how to understand the public evidence makes any reference to the kinds of cognitive abilities that humans possess. In general, though, it does seem as though the kinds of cognitive abilities that someone possesses can make a crucial difference to whether or not a given situation is evidentially ambiguous. For example, the message displayed on a road sign 50 metres away might be deeply ambiguous for someone who is severely shortsighted, but not ambiguous in the slightest for someone with 20:20 vision. I see no reason why this point wouldn't also apply to the quest for the truth about ultimate reality. After all, if God exists, God's omniscience entails that the nature of ultimate reality isn't even the tiniest bit ambiguous for God. In short, evidential ambiguity seems to be a phenomenon that is in part constituted by the cognitive limitations of a given type of finite being, or indeed, a given finite individual. When the relevant cognitive limitations are ones that are shared by the whole human species, it is quite natural for us simply to speak of the topic at issue as being ambiguous without qualifying *for whom* it is ambiguous. But I want to suggest that evidential ambiguity is, in fact, always evidential ambiguity *for someone*. In view of this point, let's proceed to consider two other ways to construe the public evidence.

One option is to identify the public evidence with the place where everyone's individual evidence overlaps, where 'everyone' means all humans and 'individual evidence' means all the information that is within a given person's purview, including all of his or her experiences, even those that are impossible to communicate to others. The difficulty with this option is that the area of overlap between everyone's individual evidence is rather meagre, just in virtue of there having been many human beings who have had a very limited range of experiences of the world. Perhaps this proposal could be finessed, so that the public evidence is identified not with the overlap of *everyone*'s individual evidence, but rather, with the overlap of the individual evidences of *all moderately well-informed people*. Or perhaps we might try to alight upon some suitably defined notion of *the average person* and thus construe the public evidence as the individual evidence of such a person. I don't want to dismiss such possible avenues, but rather than pursue them further, I would like to put forward a somewhat different proposal.

My preferred approach is to identify the public evidence with *the set of all truths that can in principle be known using widely recognised, non-inferential human cognitive abilities*. That is, I am suggesting that the public evidence – the frame of reference relative to which the answer to the worldview question is less than fully obvious – is the totality of facts that can be accessed via all of the human ways of coming to have non-inferential knowledge that almost all adult human beings would recognise as being real, which would include such cognitive abilities as vision, hearing, rational intuition, introspection, memory, and so on. Testimony is also a widely recognised way of coming to know things non-inferentially, although testimony, if it is to be a source of knowledge, must ultimately trace back to someone's use of one of the aforementioned cognitive abilities (vision, hearing, rational intuition, and so on).

It is worth noting that some of the items that are commonly treated as being part of the public evidence regarding the worldview question are facts that have been discovered through the drawing of inferences – for example, facts about the age of the universe. The facts about the age of the universe have been discovered via inferences from observations of the red-shifted quality of the light reaching us from distant galaxies, among other things (see Carr, 2008: 141–3). So, my proposed understanding of what the public evidence includes does have the result that strictly speaking those conclusions about the age of the universe that have been arrived at through inference are not part of the public evidence. What *is* part of the public evidence is the raw observational data upon which those conclusions are based, and to the extent that the inferences drawn from it are straightforward, I suggest that they can in effect be treated as part of our common stock of data for investigating the worldview question. (The following section will explore different levels or degrees of evidential ambiguity and will suggest that the public evidence regarding the worldview question is ambiguous to a greater degree than the public evidence for a typical well-confirmed scientific theory is.)

This way of delimiting the set of facts comprising the public evidence would exclude the fact that God exists if that is a fact, or the fact that all minds are material objects if that is a fact, since these aren't things that can be known non-inferentially via widely recognised human cognitive abilities. In this way, we can capture the sense that there is an important shared frame of reference – namely, the public evidence as I've just defined it – relative to which the nature of ultimate reality is not overwhelmingly obvious. Let's unpack this a bit further.

Alvin Plantinga (2000) has argued that if God exists, then that fact can be known in an instinctive way, via a kind of non-inferential cognitive faculty that God has implanted in us, which, following John Calvin, he calls the *sensus divinitatis* (sense of divinity). I don't have space here to get into discussion of Plantinga's proposal, but the 'widely recognised' qualifier in my proposed definition of the public evidence is intended to exclude from the public evidence those truths that can be known non-inferentially only by way of cognitive abilities whose existence many people do not accept. All of this is completely consistent with allowing that someone could have as part of her individual evidence truths that she has come into contact with via cognitive abilities that are not widely recognised. Indeed, it isn't at all that I am denying the existence of cognitive abilities beyond the ones with which everyone is familiar. It is simply that the shared frame of reference that we are presently trying to delineate seems best understood as excluding truths that have been arrived at via cognitive abilities that a great many people do not recognise as real. That some alleged cognitive abilities (such as a *sensus divinitatis*) are not very widely recognised presumably has to do with the way that their putative existence is tightly bound up with a comprehensive package of worldview claims.

Importantly, when I say that the public evidence is the body of facts that are knowable via non-inferential cognitive abilities that are 'widely recognised,' it isn't that the cognitive abilities in question must be ones that virtually all humans themselves possess. For example, the ability to tell precisely which species a bird belongs to by looking at its tail feathers is a cognitive ability that not many humans possess, but it is very widely accepted that some people really do have such an ability. The fact that some cognitive abilities are rare and yet widely recognised as real may have something to do with the way that their accuracy can be tested with reference to cognitive abilities that the vast majority of adult humans do possess and know how to use.

What about the fact that at different points in history, the technological and conceptual apparatus that people have had available to them has made a very significant difference to the range of facts that are accessible to them through 'ordinary human ways of knowing'? A number of authors have argued for an extended cognition thesis (Clark & Chalmers, 1998; Pritchard, 2010), according to which technological aids, including such things as eyeglasses and notebooks but perhaps also such sophisticated devices as radio telescopes and sonar systems, can be seen as a part of our cognitive abilities. I suggest that this point is easily accommodated simply by granting that the range of facts that get included in the public evidence varies over time. Some things that were not part of the public evidence during the Middle Ages – for instance, the fact that the light reaching earth from distant galaxies is red-shifted – are part of the public evidence today.

In sum, my proposed way of understanding what the public evidence consists in has the following features. It construes the public evidence as (a) a set of mind-independent facts, something that is 'out there', and something that does *not* necessarily fall within the purview of human minds; and yet as (b) something whose extent – that is, *which facts* are included in the set – is determined by the kinds of cognitive abilities that humans have. I suggest this approach offers the best way to make sense of what the philosophers quoted earlier in the section may be trying to get at with their talk of the ambiguity of the world as regards religious truth claims. That is, according to my proposed understanding, it is not ultimate reality itself that is ambiguous; rather, it is the public evidence that is ambiguous as regards the question of what ultimate reality is like.

I would also suggest that this approach fits well with the way that many have thought about what it is for an argument to count as a piece of natural theology (e.g., Plantinga, 1974: 219–20; Craig & Moreland, 2009: ix; Parsons, 2013: 247; Baker-Hytch, 2023). Natural theology has tended to be understood as the project of trying to discern or establish religious truth claims using only methods that are in some important sense religiously neutral and available in principle to all rational agents. We might say, then, that the public evidence, as I have construed it, is the raw material out of which natural theologians seek to build their arguments.

One further clarification is in order. On the understanding of evidential ambiguity being put forward in this section, evidential ambiguity pertains to propositions, agents, and sets of evidence. That is to say, a given set of evidence E is ambiguous (to some degree or other) for an agent S with respect to the truth or falsity of some proposition p. When I speak of a 'question' being evidentially ambiguous for S, what I mean is that some set of evidence E is ambiguous for some agent S with respect to the question of whether some proposition p is true or false. When I speak of a 'topic' being ambiguous, I mean that E is ambiguous for S with respect to the truth or falsity of a whole cluster of propositions pertaining to a particular subject matter. And when I speak of a 'situation' being evidentially ambiguous, I mean to refer to the whole complex of the agent(s), the proposition(s) at issue, and the set of evidence. So, to say that the public evidence is ambiguous with respect to the worldview question is to say that the public evidence (i.e., the set of all true propositions that can in principle be known using widely recognised, non-inferential human cognitive abilities) is ambiguous for human beings with respect to the truth or falsity of a whole cluster of propositions having to do with the nature of ultimate reality.

2.4 The Threefold Sources of Evidential Ambiguity

In the previous section I suggested that evidential ambiguity is always evidential ambiguity *for someone*. Again, for an omniscient being nothing could ever be evidentially ambiguous. Building on this observation, we can begin to think about what it is in the relation between an agent and the world that determines how evidentially ambiguous a given situation is for that agent (or group of agents).

It will be useful to start with a mundane example of an evidentially ambiguous situation: imagine that the couple who live on the other side of the wall from you are having an intense conversation in heightened voices in a language you don't speak, and given just the muffled tones that are audible for you through the wall, it is difficult for you to tell whether the conversation is angry or affectionate. Whether they are being affectionate or angry with one another is evidentially ambiguous for you. I want to suggest that the ambiguity arises from the interplay of three factors, namely, your *cognitive abilities*, your *vantage point*, and *the facts of the matter*. Let's consider each of these factors in turn:

1. *Cognitive abilities.* This factor includes the kinds of cognitive faculties you have, and their powers and limitations. It includes facts about what sorts of

sensory organs you have and how sensitive those sensory organs are to various kinds of stimuli. It includes facts about your capacities for drawing inferences. It includes facts about your capacities for apprehending non-empirical truths, such as truths of arithmetic, logic, and metaphysical possibility and necessity. And it includes not just facts about the biological hardware but also facts about the technological and conceptual apparatus with which you have or haven't augmented your native cognitive abilities, including whether or not you understand a given language or whether you are using things like binoculars, hearing aids, and so on. In the example, facts of this sort that are pertinent include the fact that you haven't learned to speak the language that the couple are using, the fact that you don't have the ability to see through walls (and hence cannot see the couple's facial expressions and body language), and that you can hear only those sound waves that are able to pass through the wall.

2. *Vantage point.* This is a matter of where you are positioned while you are exercising the relevant cognitive abilities, which includes the location of your body and the direction in which you are pointing your sensory organs, but potentially other factors too, such as your socio-economic position. In the example, things that are pertinent under this heading would include the fact that you're standing on the other side of the wall from the couple rather than standing in the same room as them.

3. *Facts of the matter.* This includes the facts that are in question, but also the facts about the kinds of indications and traces that are generated by the facts in question. In the example, things that fall under this heading include the fact that the couple are actually being affectionate, not angry, with one another, but that their way of talking sweetly to each other involves using elevated and urgent voices. It also includes the fact that the couple are speaking a certain language and at a certain volume, and the fact the sound waves produced by their conversation are such as to be able to travel a certain distance and be impeded to a certain degree by certain kinds of solid objects such as walls.

The interaction of these three factors might be likened to a situation involving a search of a pitch-dark room with a flashlight. The facts of the matter in question are like the contents of the pitch-dark room. Your cognitive abilities are like the flashlight, its degree of brightness and the width of its beam. And your vantage point when you exercise the relevant cognitive abilities is like your position in the room and the direction in which you're pointing the flashlight. The extent to which something is evidentially ambiguous for you, then, is a matter of the degree to which the parts of the room that you are able to illuminate are such as to yield a clear answer to some question about the contents of the room.

One might think there is a fourth factor, namely, the extent to which you have acquired defeaters concerning the matter in question. It is fairly standard in the epistemology literature to distinguish between two sorts of defeaters (Pollock, 1986), namely, undercutting defeaters, which deprive you of your reasons for believing *p* (or, at least, diminish the force of those reasons), and rebutting defeaters, which provide you with reasons for believing ¬*p*. (For discussion of the notion of defeaters and their place in epistemological theorising, see Bergmann, 1997; Lasonen-Aarnio, 2014; Baker-Hytch & Benton, 2015). The thought, then, is that whether you have acquired any defeaters concerning the proposition at issue is a further, distinct factor that can contribute to the ambiguousness of a situation, over and above the three factors already outlined. I am inclined to think, though, that this fourth factor having to do with the presence of defeaters is captured already by the conjunction of three aforementioned factors. Allow me to explain.

Imagine a situation in which you are standing in front of a Christmas market stall looking at an unopened box that has a picture of chocolates printed on the outside, and quite reasonably, you draw the conclusion that the box contains chocolates. It does in fact contain chocolates. But suppose the market stall owner confidently tells you that the box actually contains hazelnuts, not chocolates, and he doesn't seem the slightest bit insincere. Given a typical epistemological framework that involves defeaters, it is plausible that the stall owner's testimony provides you with a defeater for your belief that the box contains chocolates. You should at least become substantially less confident that it contains chocolates. But note that the fact that you were liable to acquire this defeater in the first place is due to the fact that your cognitive abilities are limited in certain ways. For example, you don't have X-ray vision so as to be able to see through the cardboard box and directly apprehend its contents within. If you did have that ability, then the stall owner's testimony wouldn't constitute a defeater for you, since you would have excellent perceptual evidence that the box does contain chocolates. Putting things more precisely, although your stock of evidence would have the stall owner's testimony added to it, your X-ray visual evidence would completely swamp that testimonial evidence.

Perhaps the most careful way to put things is to say that whether you have acquired defeaters concerning the target proposition is indeed a factor that determines how evidentially ambiguous that proposition is for you, but that the degree to which you are liable to acquire defeaters in the first place is ultimately a function of the three factors outlined earlier, namely, your cognitive abilities, your vantage point, and the facts of the matter in question. It is the interplay of these three factors that I take to be fundamental in generating evidential ambiguity. When the facts pertaining to the first and second of these factors are the same for the whole human species, it then makes sense to say that the situation is evidentially ambiguous for humans as such; indeed, it is in this sort of situation that we will tend simply to say that the situation is ambiguous, without qualifying *for whom* it is ambiguous.

2.5 Reasoning Counterfactually about Evidential Ambiguity

The threefold account just outlined may provide a helpful framework for thinking about the sources of evidential ambiguity in a given situation. Specifically, we may be able to get a better understanding of why a given situation is evidentially ambiguous by reasoning counterfactually about the minimum changes that would need to be made in any of the three respects in order for the situation to be rendered evidentially unambiguous.

Let's consider another example of a situation that is evidentially ambiguous for many of us, indeed, arguably for humans in general: the question of whether there are any extraterrestrial intelligent civilisations out there in the universe (see Vainio, 2018: ch. 5). As per the threefold account of the sources of ambiguity, the question of whether ET exists is evidentially ambiguous for us in virtue of the following factors:

1. *Cognitive abilities*: this includes facts about the powers and limitations of our sensory organs and the technological apparatus we've developed to extend those abilities, such as telescopes and radio antennae, and it includes the fact that our eyes and electronic instruments can't detect anything outside of our light cone (i.e., the region of space-time that is visible to us, given the speed at which light travels).

2. *Vantage point*: this includes facts about where our planet Earth is positioned in the Milky Way galaxy and where the Milky Way galaxy is located relative to other galaxies, and at what moment in the history of the universe the human species is located, as well as facts about the direction in which we're pointing our telescopes, radio antennae, and so on.

3. *Facts of the matter*: this includes the facts about whether there are indeed any extraterrestrial civilisations and, if so, where they are located relative to us and at what point in the history of the cosmos they emerged, how long they have been (or were) technologically advanced enough to emit electromagnetic signals, and what sorts of electromagnetic signals are (or were) generated by their activities. It also includes facts about the size of the universe.

In short, this analysis suggests that the evidential ambiguity of the question of ET's existence is traceable to the limitations of our sensory abilities – even of our technologically augmented sensory abilities, given speed-of-light constraints – in conjunction with facts about our confinement to a single vantage point in a vast cosmos. What is interesting to notice, though, is that the question of what are the minimum changes that would be needed in order for the situation to be rendered unambiguous receives different answers depending on whether ET does in fact exist or not.

If ET does in fact exist, then at least one of the following changes would be needed in order to render the situation evidentially unambiguous for us. Either, we would need to have the ability to see what is going on in spatially remote locations unmediated by the transmission of photons, so as to be able to study the surfaces of planets in far-flung galaxies without being bound by speed-of-light constraints (*cognitive abilities*); or, we would need to be located near – in astronomical terms – to a planet on which ET exists, for example, in the next solar system from us (*vantage point*); or, it would need to be the case that an extraterrestrial civilisation were broadcasting very clear signs of intelligent life within our light cone and within easily detectable portions of the electromagnetic spectrum (*the facts of the matter*).

But if ET in fact doesn't exist, then there are different answers to the question of the minimum changes that would be needed in order for the situation to be rendered unambiguous. Either, we would need to have the ability to look in every possibly inhabitable part of the universe despite its enormity, which would require more than just the ability to view distant objects unhindered by speed-of-light constraints, because the sheer number of planets in the universe would make it completely infeasible for humans to rule out ET on the basis of a planet-by-planet search – it would arguably require the ability to somehow view what's going on elsewhere in the universe all at once (*cognitive abilities*); or, it would need to be the case that the universe were small enough and contained sufficiently few planets that we could properly take ourselves to have looked everywhere using speed-of-light constrained observation methods, where 'looking' would mean something like studying the surface of all planets at the level of resolution with which we can currently study the surface of Mars (*the facts of the matter*). Arguably, given the non-existence of ET, there is no change that could be made to our *vantage point* within the universe that would render the situation less evidentially ambiguous than it actually is, given that there is no such thing as 'the centre' of the universe.

In short, in some situations, we cannot say unconditionally what are the smallest changes that would be needed in order for the situation to be evidentially unambiguous. In such situations we can only say what would need to be different conditional on the truth of a given hypothesis in order for the situation to be unambiguous.

It is plausible that the worldview question is like this: the answer to the question of the smallest changes that would be needed in order to render our situation evidentially unambiguous will be different conditional on the truth of different worldviews. A huge amount could be said about this, but let's consider just one example. Conditional on the truth of theism, perhaps the most obvious way for the question about the nature of ultimate reality to be rendered wholly unambiguous would be for humans to have a perceptual faculty that virtually all of us knew how to use and that enabled us to literally perceive God in a robust and ongoing manner, in something not too dissimilar from the way that we perceive tables and chairs. Such a perceptual ability would be very different from the fleeting and highly unpredictable mode of perception of God that William Alston (1991) alleges occasionally occurs. Conditional on the truth of naturalism, however, it isn't obvious at all whether there could be a perceptual faculty that would enable us to somehow 'see' that all that exists is ultimately physical (or is generated by that which is physical). But even if there could be such a faculty, presumably that faculty would be very different in its workings than a perceptual faculty that would enable us to perceive God's presence. The faculty for perceiving God would be putting us in direct cognitive contact with a positive feature of reality, namely, God's existence and presence. But the faculty for directly perceiving the truth of naturalism would somehow have to put us in direct cognitive contact with a universal negative truth, namely, that there are no objects or properties anywhere in reality that are supernatural. The point is simply that, as with the ET example, it looks as though there is no unconditional answer to the question of what would have to change about our situation (our cognitive faculties, our vantage point, the facts of the matter) in order for our situation regarding the worldview question to be rendered unambiguous. We can only say what would have to change given the truth of a particular worldview, or at any rate, given the truth of a particular family of worldviews, in order for the situation to be rendered wholly unambiguous. This isn't a merely theoretical point. Insofar as we have the power to bring about changes to our epistemic situation – in particular, to our cognitive abilities and the vantage point from which we are exercising those abilities – the question of *how* we ought to try to change our situation is of course going to be guided by our sense of what changes would need to be made in order to render our situation evidentially unambiguous with respect to the question at hand.

The next question is: What exactly might it mean to describe a set of evidence as ambiguous? Does it mean that the evidence is evenly balanced between two hypotheses? Or that the evidence rationally permits opposing responses? Or that the evidence is mixed in some sense? Or something else? That is the issue to which we turn in the next section.

3 Five Ways to Be Ambiguous

The previous section suggested that evidential ambiguity arises from the interplay of three factors: the cognitive abilities of an agent S; the vantage point from which S is using those cognitive abilities; and the facts of the matter in question, including the sorts of traces and indicators that are generated by those facts. The extent to which it is evidentially ambiguous for you whether or not p is true, then, is a matter of the extent to which the set of facts that you are able to grasp with your cognitive abilities given your vantage point when you are using those abilities – that is, your *evidence* – is such as to yield a clear answer to the question of whether p is true. I suggested, moreover, that the best way to make sense of the commonly held idea that the universe we inhabit is religiously ambiguous is not to suppose that reality itself is ambiguous, but instead, to suppose that there is an important shared frame of reference that is comprised of the body of facts that are in principle knowable by way of non-inferential cognitive abilities that virtually all adult humans would recognise as real – the *public evidence*, as I termed it – and that it is relative to this body of facts that the answer to the worldview question is less than fully obvious. In short, it is the public evidence, so defined, that is evidentially ambiguous with respect to the question of which worldview is true. But in what sense, exactly, can the public evidence be said to be ambiguous with respect to the worldview question? Is it that the public evidence supports competing worldviews to a roughly equal degree? Or is it that the public evidence rationally permits differing conclusions about which worldview is correct? Or something else? These are the questions that the present section is going to address.

One can discern in the recent religious epistemology literature a number of ways of thinking about what the alleged ambiguity of the public evidence regarding the worldview question might consist in. In what follows I shall evaluate five such characterisations. These characterisations come from both theists and non-theists. Notably, some of the following characterisations are more tendentious than others, which is to say, they are liable to be objectionable to adherents of some worldviews, perhaps because they presuppose the truth or probable truth of some other worldview(s). In surveying various characterisations I am particularly interested to try to find a way of characterising the ambiguity of the public evidence that satisfies two criteria.

Firstly, it should be worldview-neutral, or in other words, it shouldn't presuppose or privilege any particular worldview or family of worldviews. One reason for trying to find a worldview-neutral way of characterising the ambiguity of the public evidence is that such a characterisation might then be able to be considered as a piece of evidence in its own right that can contribute to the ongoing debates about which worldview is correct (Section 5 will consider the very question of whether evidential ambiguity itself is strong evidence for or against some worldviews).

The second criterion is that our characterisation should be genuinely interesting. There are some ways of characterising the ambiguity of the public evidence as regards the worldview question that are not very interesting, in that they also apply to the vast majority of beliefs that most of us hold about the world, including the belief that we are not being subjected to a massive and systematic deception of the sort depicted in *The Matrix*, and so on. Evidential ambiguity comes in degrees, and whilst there is perhaps a niche philosophical sense in which it is evidentially ambiguous whether or not we are victims of a Matrix-style systematic deception – the problem of radical skepticism is still a live topic within epistemology, after all – it does seem to me that the way in which the public evidence is ambiguous as regards the worldview question is somehow more substantive and interesting than that.

3.1 Characterisation #1: The Public Evidence Is Evenly Balanced

The first characterisation to consider is the idea that the public evidence supports two or more mutually exclusive worldviews to an approximately equal degree. In fact, that isn't quite the right way to put it. Two worldviews, let's call them 'A' and 'B', might be equally strongly supported by the public evidence and yet the overall situation wouldn't be significantly ambiguous if a third worldview, call it 'C', is supported vastly more strongly by the public evidence than the disjunction of all the other worldviews (including A and B) is supported by that same public evidence. So, really, the idea we are considering here is that the worldview that is most strongly supported by the public evidence, call it 'W', and the disjunction of all the logically possible worldviews that deny W, call that '¬W', are roughly equally well supported by the public evidence.

It is helpful at this point to introduce the framework that many epistemologists employ for discussing matters of evidential support, namely, Bayes' Theorem. I want to be very clear at the outset that in using Bayes' Theorem I am in no way committed to the idea that we can always assign precise numerical probabilities to propositions that have metaphysical import. In fact, I am very skeptical that we can assign precise numbers to things like the probability of there being embodied conscious agents conditional on naturalism or the probability that the God of classical theism would become incarnate. At best, we can offer vague estimates of such probabilities couched in phrases such as 'very unlikely', 'more likely than not', 'overwhelmingly likely', and so on. The benefits of using Bayes' Theorem, as I see it, are that it provides us with a framework that forces us to be transparent about various crucial assumptions in our non-deductive reasoning, it permits us to see clearly the relationship between those various assumptions, and it enables us to give careful definitions of a range of epistemologically interesting concepts.

With that large caveat out of the way, we can note that according to Bayes' Theorem, a fact E is evidence for a hypothesis H to the degree that E is more likely given H than given ¬H (the denial of H). To make this concrete with an example, the fact that John's fingerprints are all over the murder weapon (E) is evidence for the hypothesis that John is Alan's murderer (H) to the degree that E is more probable on H than it is on ¬H (the hypothesis that John is not the murderer). Where 'Prob(H|E)' means 'the probability of H conditional on E' and 'Prob(H)' means 'the probability of H', Bayes' Theorem states that

$$\text{Prob}(H|E) > \text{Prob}(H) \text{ if and only if } \text{Prob}(E|H) > \text{Prob}(E|\neg H).$$

The degree to which E is more or less likely on H than on ¬H is known as the *ratio of likelihoods*, or alternatively, as the *Bayes' factor*. The Bayes' factor is a standardly used measure of the degree to which E supports H over ¬H (for a helpful survey of various measures of the strength of evidential confirmation, see Fitelson, 2007: 478). The idea we are currently considering, then, is as follows: where 'P' is the public evidence, where 'W' is the worldview that is most strongly supported by P (as measured by the Bayes' factor), and where '¬W' is the disjunction of all the logically possible worldviews that deny W, the claim is that Prob(P|W) is approximately equal to Prob(P|¬W); or in other words, the totality of the public evidence is roughly just as likely given W as it is given ¬W; hence, W and ¬W receive roughly equal support from P.

It is surprisingly difficult to find advocates of this characterisation of evidential ambiguity in the contemporary literature. The philosopher of religion who perhaps comes closest to this way of viewing the situation is Paul Draper, but Draper's self-professed agnosticism is due to what he views as the immense difficulty of working out *where* the balance of the evidence lies:

> I believe there is plenty of clear evidence, but the clear evidence for theism is offset by the clear evidence for naturalism. I don't believe, however, that the evidence on each side is perfectly balanced, so that as a whole it has no effect on the ratio of the probability of theism to the probability of naturalism. Rather, I find it difficult to compare the strength of the various pieces of evidence. (2002: 206)

Draper, then, is not advocating the characterisation of the public evidence that we are currently considering, but one that is perhaps closer to the characterisation that we will examine in §3.4.

The 'evenly balanced' characterisation of the public evidence is worldview-neutral in one sense, namely, that it doesn't presuppose the truth of any particular worldview. But in another way it isn't neutral, because it implies something that is going to be objectionable to reflective adherents of virtually all worldviews: namely, that *no* one worldview is favoured by the overall balance of the public evidence. What's more, this is a difficult claim to establish – no less difficult than trying to establish that the public evidence favours one particular worldview over the rest. One might think that the very fact of disagreement among philosophers of religion about how to interpret the public evidence is itself strong evidence for the 'evenly balanced' claim, but as Jonathan Kvanvig points out,

> [T]hat disputes in philosophy of religion end in deadlock ... yields a bad argument for the counterbalanced claim. All the point about ending in deadlock shows is that the issues are controversial and consensus is not likely to be achieved soon. Nothing follows about the quality of the evidence for a claim just because people can't agree on what it shows. Positing the counterbalancing of the evidence might be thought to explain the disputes and their irresolvability, but it doesn't; it merely sides with some of the disputants over others. (2002: 153)

Let us turn, then, to consider a second characterisation of the ambiguity of the public evidence.

3.2 Characterisation #2: A Comparison with Moorean Beliefs and Cartesian Beliefs

The approach that we shall now consider is one that is inspired by an essay by Jason Marsh (2017). Marsh argues that religious beliefs should not be thought of as having a similar epistemic status to beliefs in 'Moorean' propositions, which is to say, humdrum propositions such as that *I have two hands* or that *it is raining*. Moorean propositions are named after the Cambridge philosopher G. E. Moore (1962: 144–8), who held that it is very easy to come by knowledge of such mundane truths. It is also very plausible that worldview beliefs do not have a similar epistemic status to beliefs in what we might term 'Cartesian' propositions, such as the proposition that *it appears that I have two hands* or that *I am having a visual experience of rain falling*. Cartesian propositions are named after René Descartes (1988 [1641]), who held that the propositions of which you can be most certain are those that describe the contents of your own mental states. The central idea with the present characterisation, then, is that there is an interesting contrast to be drawn between worldview beliefs that are based on the public evidence and our beliefs about these two other important classes of propositions. To begin with, we need to say a bit more about these two classes of propositions.

A Cartesian proposition, we might say, is a proposition describing the contents of one's own mind. Examples of Cartesian propositions would be the proposition that *I'm in pain* or *I'm having an auditory experience of an orchestra playing a symphony*. Because of the fact that these are the sorts of propositions that I have access to just by inspecting the contents of my own mind, Descartes thought that their truth couldn't be doubted by me. The evidence for a Cartesian proposition is simply one's *being in* the mental state that the proposition describes. The evidence that I am in pain is simply my *being in pain*. Timothy Williamson (2000: 93–113) has notably contested the idea that any mental state is 'luminous,' in other words, is such that one is always in a position to know whether one is in that mental state. Williamson's rejection of the luminosity of our own mental states in turn leads him to reject the idea that there is some special class of propositions pertaining to our inner states whose truth cannot be doubted. But even if Williamson's objections go through, it is plausible that our epistemic position in relation to propositions about the contents of our own minds is very strong indeed; arguably, the evidential situation we are in with respect to such propositions is about as unambiguous as it gets.

Moorean propositions are propositions that describe more than merely the contents of our own minds. They describe a reality outside of our own minds, but they are such that outside a philosophy seminar room virtually no one seriously doubts them. Such propositions are often described as items of 'commonsense.' Examples would include the propositions that *I have two hands*, that *it is sunny outside,* that *the law of gravity will still be operating next week*, and that *Jane is sad* (based on observing her melancholic facial expressions). Moore (1962: 144–8) claimed that the conjunction of the premises of any skeptical argument that tries to deny that we can know such propositions is always going to be less plausible than the claim that we do indeed know such propositions. I suggest that all the examples of Moorean propositions just given seem to have the following characteristics, where *p* is the proposition at issue and S is the person who believes *p*:

(i) *p* strongly seems to S to be true. On some accounts of evidence, it follows from this that S has good evidence for believing *p* (for discussion of such an approach to epistemology, known as 'phenomenal conservatism,' see Tucker, 2013).

(ii) Relatedly, it comes naturally to humans to strongly believe p in an instinctive, non-inferential manner when faced with certain sorts of everyday experiences. In the language of cognitive science, believing p is 'maturationally natural' for developmentally normal humans (McCauley, 2011).

(iii) The fact that p describes more than merely the way things appear to S – more than merely the contents of S's own mental states – means that p suffers from a certain kind of evidential underdetermination. For example, the fact that it visually appears to S that she has two hands is logically compatible with her not having any hands; it is logically possible, that is, that S is a handless brain in a vat being fed illusory visual experiences of having hands. This is what distinguishes Cartesian propositions from Moorean propositions. It has been common to suppose that when it comes to Cartesian propositions, the way things appear to S is sufficient to guarantee the truth of the proposition (though for arguments against this, see Bergmann, 2021: 95–103). But with Moorean propositions, the way things appear to S isn't sufficient to guarantee the truth of the proposition. Hence why Moorean beliefs can seem to be threatened by the logical possibility of radically deceptive scenarios in a way that Cartesian beliefs are not (see Pritchard, 2005: ch. 4).

(iv) In the typical case, S will be aware of no strong evidence against p. Importantly, just because S's belief in p suffers from the aforementioned evidential underdetermination, it doesn't follow that S has any evidence *against p*. Let p be the proposition that *I have two hands*. Ordinarily, there will be no proposition E within S's total evidence such that E is strong evidence against p. In rare cases, S might acquire some evidence for thinking that she is being subjected to some kind of localised perceptual illusion, such as a convincing hologram or a trick of the light. Such cases are rare in everyday life, and typically it is easy for S to investigate whether she is indeed being subjected to some such localised perceptual illusion so as to decisively confirm or disconfirm the possibility.

So, the suggestion that we are currently considering is that worldview beliefs that are based only on the public evidence are epistemically not on a par with Cartesian beliefs or Moorean beliefs; their epistemic status is weaker than either of these two classes of belief. This is another possible way to characterise the evidential ambiguity pertaining to the worldview question.

Why think worldview beliefs that are based only on the public evidence are not on a par with Cartesian beliefs? Put simply, propositions such as *God exists* or *all minds are material objects* or *human souls are reincarnated after death* describe more than merely the way that things appear to some human agent S; they describe more than merely the contents of someone's own mental states. Beliefs about such propositions therefore suffer from the aforementioned evidential underdetermination that equally afflicts the belief that *I have two hands*.

Perhaps more interestingly, why think worldview beliefs that are based only on the public evidence are not epistemically on a par with Moorean beliefs? To examine this question, we need to work through the four features of Moorean beliefs that I enumerated earlier. Beliefs about worldview propositions such as *God exists* or *all minds are material objects* or *human souls are reincarnated after death* often have feature (i) in common with paradigm examples of Moorean beliefs. Some such beliefs have characteristic (ii) in common with paradigm examples of Moorean belief. Reformed Epistemologists have argued that belief in God is similar to paradigm Moorean beliefs in being a belief that comes naturally to human beings (Plantinga, 2000: 175–7; Clark & Barrett, 2011). Many worldview beliefs are not like this, though – for example, the belief that *there is a God who is three persons and one substance* does not come naturally to humans. As just noted, worldview beliefs also have feature (iii) in common with Moorean beliefs; worldview beliefs are subject to evidential underdetermination.

So far, then, we have seen good reasons to regard at least some worldview beliefs, though by no means all, as being very much like Moorean beliefs with respects to features (i), (ii), and (iii). Things sharply diverge, however, when we come to feature (iv). Unlike paradigm Moorean beliefs, one's worldview beliefs are usually such that one is aware of some item(s) of evidence that taken in isolation would fairly strongly disconfirm the worldview proposition at issue. For theists, that might well be the evidence of widespread suffering. For naturalists, it might be evidence of apparent design in the cosmos. To be clear, I'm not saying anything here about whether the total public evidence ultimately favours theism or naturalism, but just that there are subsets of the public evidence that taken in isolation would count against either of these worldviews. In short, this is what makes beliefs in worldview propositions different from beliefs in propositions such as that *I have two hands*.

This way of characterising the ambiguity of the public evidence as regards the worldview question is fairly worldview-neutral. It doesn't obviously presuppose or favour any particular worldview. However, for the evidence for a given proposition to be ambiguous in this sense is arguably not all that interesting, given that the vast majority of propositions in the domains of science and history are also subject to this kind of evidential ambiguity. To take just one example, the proposition that *the earth is much more than a few thousand years old* is neither a Cartesian proposition nor a Moorean proposition, but the evidence for it is overwhelmingly strong – it is not evidentially ambiguous in a very interesting sense. For that reason, we shall now turn to look at some characterisations that don't apply nearly so widely, and that arguably do pick out genuinely interesting senses in which the public evidence might be said to be ambiguous as regards the worldview question.

3.3 Characterisation #3: The Public Evidence Can Reasonably Be Interpreted in Mutually Incompatible Ways

Consider the following passages from essays by John Hick, Robert McKim, and T. J. Mawson:

> By the religious ambiguity of the universe I do not mean that it has no definite character but that it is capable from our present human vantage point of being thought and experienced in both religious and naturalistic ways. (Hick, 1989: 73)

> The world manifests ambiguity in that it is open both to secular and to religious readings, but also in that it is open to a number of religious readings. (McKim, 2001: 22)

> I think that many of these arguments [for theism] do in fact do something to raise the probability of there being a God on their premises, premises which are themselves at least somewhat more plausible than their negations. But I'd also concede that there's no one 'killer fact', e.g., a fact that everyone agrees is a fact; that everyone can see needs explanation; and that obviously needs God for its explanation. *It's not that atheists are simply missing something obvious*. (Mawson, 2013: 25, emphasis mine)

To be sure, none of these three authors explicitly says that two mutually incompatible interpretations of the public evidence can both be reasonable, but that does seem fairly implicit in the preceding quotations, and that is the suggestion that we shall now consider.

Such a characterisation of the public evidence presupposes a thesis about the nature of rationality known as *rational permissivism*. Rational permissivism says that there are some bodies of evidence that are such that more than one rational doxastic attitude is possible in response to that evidence (where a doxastic attitude could be a belief that p or something more fine-grained such as a 65% credence in p). Consider a case where two jurors are confronted with the very same body of evidence in a murder trial and come to opposite conclusions about whether the defendant is guilty. If it is true that both jurors have exactly the same evidence as one another and that both are rational in arriving at their conclusions, it follows that rational permissivism is true. The converse view, that at most one rational doxastic attitude is possible in response to a given body of evidence, is known as the rational uniqueness thesis. If rational permissivism isn't what is in view in the preceding quotations, then it is hard to think what else could be in view other than the idea that the public evidence is approximately evenly balanced, which collapses into characterisation #1. So, for the sake of exploring a distinct view, I shall assume that characterisation #3 does imply rational permissivism.

Its presupposing rational permissivism doesn't prevent characterisation #3 from being worldview-neutral, but it does make it controversial to the extent that rational permissivism is a contested view in epistemology (for an overview of the current debate around rational permissivism and rational uniqueness, see Kopec & Titelbaum, 2016).

It is important to note that there are broadly two versions of rational permissivism on the table. *Intrapersonal* permissivism says that there is more than one rationally permissible doxastic attitude that one and the same agent S might have towards the proposition p on the basis of a body of evidence E. For example, according to intrapersonal permissivism there might be a situation in which it would be just as rationally permissible for S to believe p on the basis of E as it would for S to believe $\neg p$ on the basis of E. By contrast, *interpersonal* permissivism says that in some situations it is rationally permissible for two distinct agents, S1 and S2, to have different doxastic attitudes towards p on the basis of a body of evidence E. This latter version does not imply that there is more than one rational doxastic attitude that S1 could have towards p, nor does it imply that there is more than one rational doxastic attitude that S2 could have towards p. Intrapersonal permissivism seems more vulnerable than interpersonal permissivism to the sort of objection that has been levelled by Roger White (2005), according to which rational permissivism has the unwelcome result that you would do just as well to flip a coin to decide what to believe about whether p is true as you would to try to work out what to believe on the basis of evidence. This does seem like a genuine worry for intrapersonal permissivism, given its allowance that one and the same person could be just as rational in believing p on the basis of E as she would be in believing $\neg p$ on the basis of E. But interpersonal permissivism isn't committed to claiming that one and the same person could have more than one rational doxastic attitude open to her/him.

Let's consider interpersonal permissivism a bit more closely. Subjective Bayesianism is a notable version of interpersonal permissivism (see Kvanvig, 2002: 150–3). Subjective Bayesianism says that two agents, S1 and S2, might start out with different prior probability functions that are both rationally permissible, where a prior probability function is a set of propositions of the form *the prior probability of there being a God is .0001* or *the probability of there being conscious agents conditional on naturalism is extremely low.* A complete prior probability function would specify an unconditional prior probability – that is, a prior probability conditional on nothing but logical truths – for every proposition there is, and a conditional prior probability – that is, a statement of the form *the probability of p conditional on q is 60%* – for every pair of propositions there is. Of course, there are vastly many propositions that you have never even thought of, let alone consciously assigned a probability to. It is a debated question whether or not we implicitly assign probabilities even to propositions that we have never consciously considered. It is also debated whether we have sharp credences, for example, that would assign a probability of 88.5% to a given proposition, or merely vague credences, such as that a given proposition is overwhelmingly probable. The only rational requirement that subjective Bayesianism places on your prior probability function is that it be internally coherent. The idea, then, is that when S1 and S2 are presented with a given bit of evidence E, adding E to their overall stocks of evidence may make different conclusions about *p* rational for each of them because of their different prior probability functions. Something like this picture is perhaps the best way to make sense of the idea that the ambiguity of the public evidence consists in its being rationally permissive.

Arguably the most plausible versions of permissivism hold that not all evidential situations are rationally permissive, and that it is only situations with certain characteristics that are rationally permissive. What might those characteristics be? The evidence being roughly evenly balanced in its support for two or more competing hypotheses? Perhaps that's one way, but if that's the only way, then characterisation #3 just collapses into characterisation #1. Another way for an evidential situation to be rationally permissive, perhaps, is for the body of evidence under consideration to be very large and complex. Yet another way might be for the evidence to be mixed, in a certain sense. Let's proceed, then, to consider two further characterisations of evidential ambiguity that make reference to these features.

3.4 Characterisation #4: The Body of Facts that Comprises the Public Evidence Is Very Large and Complex

In a thoughtful piece reflecting on the epistemology of arriving at a worldview, William Abraham makes the astute observation that

> [T]he weighing of evidence in this instance cuts across a whole network of data and warrants ... [T]he full articulation of the grounds for our favoured

metaphysical vision is unlikely to be executed by any single individual ...
There is simply no way in which one can be a kind of Renaissance or
Enlightenment rationalist who covers all the relevant data and warrants.
(1987: 35–36)

It seems as though it should be fairly uncontroversial that the public evidence
pertaining to the worldview question is indeed very complex and spans numerous areas of expertise. Among other things, the public evidence includes all the
following:

- facts relevant to the age and origins of the universe, its fundamental laws,
  initial conditions, and its development from its earlier states to its present
  state;
- facts relevant to the origins of life from non-life and the development and
  emergence of increasingly complex life forms;
- facts pertaining to the structure and functioning of the human brain and its
  correlations with conscious experience;
- facts about moral value and obligation (or perhaps more minimally, facts
  about our intuitions concerning moral value and obligation);
- facts about modal logic and facts about what is metaphysically necessary and
  what is metaphysically possible;
- facts about suffering and its intensity, distribution, and kinds, and the struc-
  tural connections between various types of good states of affairs and evil
  states of affairs;
- facts about the contents of human meta-normal experiences, including what
  are sometimes termed 'religious experiences' and 'spiritual experiences',
  where the relevant descriptions of such experiences have the worldview-
  neutral form, 'Ted had an experience in which it seemed to him that an
  infinitely light and loving presence filled the room', or 'after the five minutes
  during which her heart was stopped Jane had the clear memory of having had
  an experience (during the five minutes in which her heart was stopped) in
  which it seemed to her that she floated above her body and observed the
  surgical procedures being carried out on her';
- facts about the historical events as a result of which the various world
  religions came into existence and spread;
- facts about the contents of human religious and irreligious beliefs and their
  distribution across time and space.

The sheer quantity of data here and the vast web of explanatory relationships
between so many of these facts is rather bewildering. One way to frame the kind
of ambiguity that might be thought to consist in the sheer scale and complexity
of the evidence here is simply to suggest that there is an information-processing

challenge: human cognitive abilities are pushed to their very limits in the attempt to take stock of this huge body of data of so many kinds and to draw judicious inferences from it with regard to the worldview question.

Characterisation #4 seems to be worldview-neutral. There is no sense in which this way of describing the situation presupposes or privileges any particular worldview, as far as I can see. But a couple of rather interesting things are suggested by this characterisation. Firstly, it suggests that coming to an accurate overall judgment about which way the total public evidence points is going to be challenging. Secondly, it raises a question about whether coming to an overall judgment about the total evidence is best done by trying to 'add up' lots of smaller sub-judgments using some aggregation framework or instead whether some kind of impressionistic, holistic judgment is called for. We'll return to these questions in the next section. Finally, the fact that there's so much relevant evidence pertaining to the worldview question suggests that certain portions of the evidence could easily be overlooked by someone, and not necessarily culpably so. This could allow for rational divergence of opinion that doesn't require rational permissivism to be true – that is, different people could rationally come to different conclusions simply because they have been exposed to different portions of the public evidence.

3.5 Characterisation #5: The Public Evidence Is Mixed

Let's turn finally to a characterisation of the public evidence as being ambiguous in virtue of being *mixed*, in a certain sense. The sense I am interested in is one that has been outlined in the following passage by Charity Anderson:

> Suppose we make a natural division of our evidence into pieces (where a piece is either a proposition or a conjunction of propositions). We rely on context to make judgments about which pieces are relevant to our topic. Call our evidence 'mixed' when the following is true: there is some relevant piece such that if that piece were our total evidence, God's existence would be likely relative to that piece; and there is some relevant piece such that were that piece our total evidence, God's existence would be unlikely relative to it. (2021: 12)

A body of evidence which is mixed in this sense might be characterised formally like so, where E is the total relevant evidence that bears upon some hypothesis H, e_1 is a proper subset of E, e_2 is another proper subset of E, and e_1 is not identical with e_2:

$Prob(e_1|H) > Prob(e_1|\neg H)$, and $Prob(e_2|H) < Prob(e_2|\neg H)$.

In other words, e_1 is more likely on H than on ¬H, and e_2 is more likely on ¬H than on H. Thus, e_1 and e_2 could be said to be pointing in opposite directions.

A very important point to note is that E's being mixed in this sense does *not* entail that E lends equal or nearly equal support to H and to ¬H alike. Specifically, E's being mixed in the preceding sense is fully compatible with e_1 lending substantially more support to H than e_2 lends to ¬H. E's being mixed is also compatible with E containing other proper subsets besides e_1 and e_2, where these other subsets lend substantial support to H over ¬H. Hence, characterisation #5 doesn't collapse into characterisation #1. At the same time, if characterisation #5 is to be really interesting, E's being mixed needs to consist in there being at least one proper subset of E that, when taken in isolation, at least *fairly strongly* supports H, and there being at least one other proper subset of E that, when taken in isolation, at least *fairly strongly* supports ¬H.

The following is an example of a body of evidence that is mixed in this interesting sense. The example, which sensitive readers may wish to skip over, is a real-life investigative cold case involving the suspicious deaths of an elderly couple in their home in the town of Wilmslow, England some twenty-four years ago (Collins, 2022). The wife was very clearly murdered, but the cause of the husband's violent death was the focus of intense scrutiny. Did the husband murder his wife and then take his own life? Or was there a third-party killer who was responsible for murdering both the husband and wife and staging the crime scene to look like a murder-suicide? The evidence relevant to this question included all the following items:

(A) The forensic investigators were unable to find any clear signs that a third-party intruder had entered the house during the relevant timeframe, despite conducting a very meticulous inch-by-inch search of the house, albeit with the forensics techniques available in 1999;

(B) the husband's blood was found on the outside of the knife drawer in the kitchen;

(C) the husband's DNA was found on the weapon used to murder the wife;

(D) the husband's hands and forearms bore injuries of the kind typical of an attempt to protect oneself against a knife-wielding attacker;

(E) the blood patterning and the positioning of the husband's body were very difficult to make sense of unless the body had been repositioned after the husband was already dead;

(F) the husband had received two separate mortal injuries, each of which would normally be individually sufficient to bring about death almost immediately, and of a kind that would be physically impossible to carry out on oneself simultaneously;

(G) three years earlier, in the same town, another elderly couple died in strikingly similar circumstances, even down to the exact positioning of the bodies in the marital bed, and yet the media reporting on that earlier case had included nothing beyond a very brief and generic account which stated that a murder-suicide of an elderly couple had occurred in the town of Wilmslow.

(A), (B), and (C) comprise a subset of the total evidence that strongly supports the hypothesis that the husband murdered his wife before taking his own life. And yet (D), (E), (F), and (G) form another subset that even more strongly supports the hypothesis that there was a third-party killer. Arguably, the overall balance of the evidence at least modestly – although I would suggest, quite strongly – favours the third-party killer hypothesis. But given the way in which different portions of the evidence point in such bewilderingly different directions, it is somewhat understandable why various investigators might have ended up coming to differing conclusions about this puzzling case, as indeed they did. This evidence seems to exhibit the property of being mixed in a very interesting sense indeed, and yet – or so it seems to me – the evidence is far from being evenly balanced between the two hypotheses.

The notion of a set of evidence being mixed in the sense we are considering seems to be true of the public evidence regarding the worldview question. Indeed, some reflective theists readily grant that the facts of evil and suffering, when taken in isolation, are strong evidence against theism (Benton, Hawthorne, & Isaacs, 2016). Some non-theists admit that facts about the apparent order and structure in the natural world, including the fine-tuning of the universe, are strong evidence against naturalism, when taken in isolation (Draper, 2002: 199–200).

Characterisation #5 seems to be a worldview-neutral way of characterising the evidential ambiguity of the public evidence. It ought to be acceptable to adherents of a wide range of worldviews, including those who think that the balance of the public evidence ultimately favours their preferred worldview. What's more, it is genuinely interesting: not just any set of evidence is mixed in the sense just outlined. The total evidence pertaining to a typical, well-confirmed scientific theory is not mixed in this sense. Just to take one example, the theory that the universe was in an extremely hot and dense state in the very distant past is strongly supported by various lines of evidence, including the way in which the light from distant galaxies is red-shifted, indicating that they are moving away from our own galaxy, and the presence of microwave background radiation that is uniformly distributed throughout the observable universe, which is the remnant of an extremely hot, dense state in the distant cosmic past (Carr, 2008: 141–3). The total evidence relevant to this theory contains no subset that supports the falsity of this theory anywhere near as strongly as the positive evidence supports its truth, and hence the evidence is not mixed in the sense that we have been considering here.

3.6 An Interesting and Worldview-Neutral Characterisation

I have suggested that a worldview-neutral characterisation of the ambiguity of the public evidence regarding the worldview question, and one that is really interesting in the sense of not applying to a whole lot of propositions in domains such as history and the natural sciences, includes the following points.

The public evidence is extremely extensive and complex and spans many areas of expertise, such that no one individual can hope to gain firsthand familiarity with all or most of it. All of this raises difficult questions about how one ought to go about attempting to arrive at an overall judgment about what the total public evidence supports. The scale and complexity of the public evidence also suggests that there may well be situations in which agents rationally arrive at differing conclusions simply in virtue of being exposed to different portions of the total public evidence, perhaps non-culpably, and without rational permissivism needing to be true.

The public evidence is mixed, in the sense that it contains at least one proper subset that fairly strongly supports one worldview and at least one other proper subset that fairly strongly supports another, mutually incompatible worldview. This characterisation is compatible with its being the case that one worldview is on balance better supported than other worldviews by the total public evidence. The fact that adherents of the various major worldviews have invested extensive time and effort into attempting to reconcile certain portions of the public evidence with their favoured worldview implicitly testifies to the mixed nature of the public evidence. Theists have devoted huge energy to attempting to reconcile the existence of an omnipotent and omnibenevolent God with the amounts and kinds of evil in our world. Naturalists have devoted massive resources to attempting to explain away features of the world that seem on the face of it to point towards intentional design. Adherents of monistic pantheism (e.g., Advaita Vedanta) have devoted intense thought to the question of why there appears to be ontological plurality in the world (see Dalal, 2021).

As far as I can see, all the above points could be accepted by someone who believes that the overall balance of the total public evidence ultimately favours their worldview over the alternatives. The preceding points are also entirely consistent with the possibility that some people are individually in possession of evidence that points overwhelmingly and unambiguously to the truth of a particular worldview, perhaps through having had overwhelmingly powerful religious experiences. Put another way, everything I have said is fully consistent with the thought that some people's evidence includes much more than just the public evidence. The point is simply that the public evidence – the body of public facts that can be apprehended using widely recognised human cognitive abilities – constitutes an important shared frame of reference relative to which the answer to the worldview question is ambiguous in at least the ways just sketched.

4 Seeking Truth amidst Ambiguity

The question of how we should go about investigating the nature of ultimate reality is far from trivial. Some theists will want to make room for apparent experiences of God's presence to feature prominently in the quest for the truth about ultimate reality, perhaps because they believe that the clearest way for us to apprehend that reality would be for us to have a direct perceptual awareness of God. Naturalists, by contrast, are often uneasy about giving much evidential weight to the contents of such reported religious experiences, tending to worry that the human mind has more than enough in the way of mechanisms capable of generating illusory experiences of a transcendent realm that nevertheless feel enormously compelling. This is but one example of many of the controversies that pertain to the question of how we should investigate ultimate reality.

Difficulties in working out how to conduct the investigation might well be seen as another characteristic of an evidentially ambiguous situation, in addition to those characteristics that we explored in Section 3. When a situation is evidentially entirely unambiguous, the question of how to go about investigating and how much weight to assign various kinds of evidence doesn't really arise. There isn't any serious question or dispute about how to find out approximately what shape the earth is. By contrast, there is a serious question about how to investigate whether any extraterrestrial intelligent civilisations exist. There is a serious question, for example, about the extent to which eyewitness reports of alleged UFOs that are hard to explain as terrestrial objects should be given much evidential weight, or whether the failure of SETI thus far to pick up any clearly intelligence-originating signals should be seen as strong evidence against extraterrestrial intelligence (see Vainio, 2018: ch. 5). Similarly, there is a serious question about how to investigate whether some kind of afterlife awaits us on the other side of the grave. There is a serious question, for example, about whether to give substantial weight to the numerous reported cases of

Near-Death Experiences in which someone has lucid conscious experiences and sometimes even apparent perceptual awareness of events that can be independently corroborated, despite having no heartbeat or detectable brain activity during the time when the experience occurred (see Allison, 2022: chs. 7–8). Perhaps all this is related to the point that was explored in §2.5, where I suggested that we can't give an unconditional answer to the question of what would need to be different in order for our epistemic situation with respect to the worldview question to be rendered wholly unambiguous. The answer to the question of the smallest changes that would be needed in order for our situation to be rendered evidentially unambiguous will be different conditional on the truth of different worldviews. As I stressed in §2.5, this isn't a merely theoretical point, because insofar as we have the power to bring about changes to our epistemic situation – in particular, to our cognitive abilities and the vantage point from which we are exercising those abilities – the question of *how* we ought to try to change our situation is of course going to be guided by our sense of what changes would need to be made in order to render our situation evidentially unambiguous with respect to the question at hand.

In the contemporary religious epistemology literature we can make out broadly two families of views about how one ought to investigate the worldview question, to which I'll give the labels *the involved approach* and *the detached approach*. To lump the various views on offer under these two headings is of course a simplification, and in reality the situation is perhaps more like a spectrum than a binary. Nonetheless, it seems to me that we can usefully group the approaches into these two camps without too much loss for our present purposes. The involved approach, then, claims roughly that the only way to obtain the best and most decisive evidence about the nature of ultimate reality is in some sense to 'step inside' a specific worldview by inhabiting its associated praxis, allowing one's desires and affections to be shaped by its way of seeing the world, perhaps even yielding one's will in some way. The detached approach, by contrast, claims that the only proper way to gather evidence about the worldview question and rationally arrive at a conclusion about which way that evidence points is to employ a quasi-scientific methodology that strives to be as impartial as possible. The present section will attempt to offer an evaluation of these two approaches and to propose something of a hybrid of both.

4.1 Some Varieties of the Involved Approach

The involved approach takes its cue from historical thinkers in the philosophico-theological tradition such as Blaise Pascal (1995 [1669]), William James (1979 [1896]), John Henry Newman (1872), and Samson Raphael Hirsch (1960

[1836]). Advocates of the involved approach often appeal to a couple of considerations that are intended to cast doubt on the value of the detached approach. For one thing, some allege that theoretical arguments for the existence of God (or, indeed, for non-theistic views of the nature of ultimate reality) rarely succeed in swaying people, and that the actual function of such arguments is simply to confirm prior commitments (Cottingham, 2005: ch. 1). Or, put even more strongly, the claim might be that the detached approach is a pretence and the involved approach is truer to how humans beings actually operate. For another thing, advocates of the involved approach often contend that the leading arguments for the existence of God, even if successful, don't establish the existence of a being who is worthy of worship. The currently popular fine-tuning argument, for example, at best establishes that there is some kind of intelligent agency responsible for calibrating the constants and initial conditions of the universe, or so the thought goes. The argument from contingency at best establishes that there is a necessary being. And so on. But all of this is unsatisfying according to various advocates of the involved approach, given that the worship-worthiness of God occupies such a central place in the life of many religious traditions (Moser, 2010: ch. 3).

Three contemporary philosophers, namely, Paul Moser, John Cottingham, and Mark Wynn, could all be seen as advocates of some variety or other of the involved approach. The work of these three philosophers bears out some common themes but also some notable differences of emphasis. In particular, they are by no means of the same mind on the question of how worthwhile it is to engage in the project of natural theology, that is, the exploration of philosophical arguments about the nature of ultimate reality that start from premises that are supposed to be broadly acceptable independently of one's prior worldview commitments. Moser (2010) is perhaps the most pessimistic about the value of natural theology, whilst Wynn (1999) has himself engaged in natural theology, offering among other things fresh renditions of arguments for theism from aesthetic and moral value in the world. Even so, it is notable that the kinds of natural theological arguments Wynn has developed are those that appeal to aspects of human experience that are less amenable to descriptions in purely scientific, third-personal terms. It is worth briefly pausing to look at what each of these three authors has to say about the way in which the worldview question should be approached.

A central contention in the work of Moser (2004, 2010) is that the God of Judeo-Christian theism, possessing the attributes of personhood and perfect love, would have no reason to offer humans mere 'spectator' evidence, by which Moser means the sort of evidence that can be weighed dispassionately as one might weigh the evidence concerning the existence of a hypothetical sub-atomic particle. Instead, such a God would offer 'authoritative' evidence, which has the following characteristics: (i) such evidence can be obtained only by willingly submitting to God as Lord, that is, as morally authoritative over one's life; (ii) such evidence consists primarily of the sense of conviction of one's moral failures through one's conscience, and secondarily of the trans-formation of one's character that results from yielding to God's offer of for-giveness and grace. Moser's epistemology thus flows from his view of the manner in which a God of the sort depicted in the Judeo-Christian scriptures would wish for humans to have epistemic access to God.

Cottingham's (2005) approach is not greatly dissimilar, but his starting point is the thought that there are certain kinds of truths – including some truths that don't directly pertain to the worldview question – which cannot be grasped purely intellectually. Cottingham appeals to Martha Nussbaum's (1990: 262–9) discussion of a character in one of Proust's novels who tries to engage in a dispassionate analysis of his own inner state to work out if he loves a woman named Albertine, and he concludes he doesn't. But then Albertine leaves town one day and he is engulfed with an anguish that tells him quite clearly that he does love her. Cottingham suggests that many of the central claims made by the major religions are like this in terms of our epistemic access to them, and he dwells particularly on the Christian doctrine of the Incarnation. As he puts it, 'The unavoidable nature of our human predicament is that we can only learn through a certain degree of receptivity, by to some extent letting go, by reaching out in trust' (2005: 17). The only way to properly assess the truth of a religious worldview, then, is to allow oneself to be open to its way of seeing the world, which includes allowing one's affections to be shaped by its practices and its liturgies. Crucial to Cottingham's approach is the thought that the affections or emotions are not mere reactions to valueless stimuli; rather, the emotions are actually capable of putting us in contact with objective features of reality that are otherwise inaccessible to us.

Wynn's (2005) epistemology of religious belief develops in considerable depth the idea that the emotions can disclose objective truths about value that we cannot otherwise access. According to his account, the emotions can actually constitute a form of veridical perception of reality. A striking example drawn from Peter Goldie (2000: 59–60) that Wynn (2005: 98) discusses is the way in which a person might experience black ice very differently before and after a nasty fall on some such ice. Before the accident, the person will of course have the theoretical belief that black ice is dangerous, but after the accident she will actually have a superior cognitive grasp of what black ice is. Wynn's suggestion is that what is different now is that her emotions are enabling her to grasp the property of the black ice's dangerousness in a way she didn't before, making the presence of black ice newly salient in her perceptual field. We might say that her emotional involvement with black ice through having a nasty fall upon it enables her to apprehend black ice in a new way, one that isn't easily articulable in words. Emotions, on this view, can have intentional content; they can put us in cognitive contact with objective features of reality, especially moral and aesthetic values. Part of Wynn's project is to suggest that a number of familiar topics in the philosophy of religion are seen in a new light if we accept this epistemological sensibility concerning the emotions. He writes that, '[P]erhaps theistic experience can be understood (in some cases anyway) as a kind of affectively toned sensitivity to the values that 'make up' God's reality?' (2005: 5). In particular, Wynn is keen to stress that emotionally infused experience can serve as a legitimate starting point for inquiry into the nature of ultimate reality:

> I suggest, then, that it is practically rational to allow ourselves to be governed by affectively toned, implicational [i.e., holistic] readings of experience in the first instance … [W]e could say that our theoretical enquiries into the ultimate character of the world have to be embedded within some prior sense of the existential meaning of experience, where this prior sense is properly taken as prima facie justified. (2005: 137–8)

Accordingly, Wynn (2009, 2020) has gone on to develop careful accounts of the ways in which paying attention to religiously significant places and participating in traditions that aim to form our moral characters can enable us to make cognitive contact with reality in ways that wouldn't otherwise be possible.

4.2 The Conditional Importance of the Involved Approach

I want to make the suggestion that the involved approach – or at least, some elements of it – probably is required for attaining the fullest picture of the nature of ultimate reality conditional on the truth of some worldviews, but that it probably isn't needed for getting the fullest picture of things conditional on the truth of some other worldviews. Again, this relates to the point I made in §2.5, that the answer to the question of what are the smallest changes that would be needed in order for our evidential situation to be rendered unambiguous will be different conditional on the truth of different worldviews. Specifically, what I want to suggest now is that conditional on the truth of theistic worldviews, something of the involved approach is probably needed for attaining the clearest view of ultimate reality that we can hope to have ante-mortem. The reason for this has to do the way in which ultimate reality is personal, given theism, and with the way that knowledge of persons has some distinctive characteristics.

There has been a recent spate of interest in the topic of knowledge of persons, with particularly notable contributions by Eleonore Stump (2010: chs. 3–4) and Matthew Benton (2017). Both authors make what I view as a powerful case for supposing that knowledge of persons is distinct from and irreducible to knowledge of propositions. Stump makes the case for the irreducibility of interpersonal knowledge to propositional knowledge in part by appealing to thought experiments. One such thought experiment is an adaptation of Frank Jackson's (1986) well-known 'Mary's room' case, in which a brilliant scientist named Mary has learned all there is to know about the physical properties of red light and its effects upon the retina, the optic nerve, the visual cortex, and so on. Despite this exhaustive physical under-standing of red light and of the neurobiology of seeing red, Mary has never herself had a visual experience of a red object. When one day she sees a red object for the very first time in her life, it seems very plausible that there is a property that she encounters anew. But since she was already completely familiar with all the physical properties of red light and of the neurobio-logical processes involved with human perception of red light, we seem to be pushed to conclude that that property she encounters for the first time – what it's like to see red – is not a physical property. In Stump's adaptation (2010: 50–3), Mary has access to all the information about the world that is expressible in third-person propositional form. Mary has never in her life had a personal interaction with another human being. Then one day Mary is rescued from her isolation by her mother, who loves her very much. As she begins to form a personal relationship with her mother there are all sorts of things she learns, including what it is like to be loved, to be hugged, to be looked in the eye, and so on. Stump contends that this thought experiment 'can support the intuition that knowledge of persons is no more expressible as knowledge *that* than first-person knowledge of color gained through perception is' (2010: 52).

Benton (2017) adduces a wealth of data in support of the distinctiveness and irreducibility of interpersonal knowledge. To begin with, he notes that many natural languages actually use different verbs for propositional know-ledge and for firsthand familiarity with a thing or person, strongly suggest-ing that there is widespread recognition of the difference. English doesn't use different verbs, but it is clear nonetheless that English grammatically marks the division between these distinct kinds of knowledge. For example, Benton (2017: 816) notes that it looks very much like there are two meanings of 'know' at issue in the first of the following pair of sentences, which cannot be collapsed into a single meaning of 'know' as the second sentence attempts to do:

(i) Hannah knows that penguins waddle, and Ted knows John
(ii) Hannah knows that penguins waddle, and Ted, John

Similarly, Benton (2017: 817) points out that the following sentence tries to use a single meaning of 'know' when in fact two different meanings of 'know' are in play, and thus the sentence sounds bizarre:

(iii) Elise knows Susan better than that the Yankees won.

In addition to discussing a great deal of linguistic data, Benton also offers various cases that support the intuition that propositional knowledge is fundamentally different from interpersonal knowledge. In one such case, Juan and Julia attend the same large committee meetings over the course of many years and have learned many propositions about one another and yet they have never interacted with one another in the sense of addressing one another directly. Whilst they have large amounts of knowledge-*that* about one another, they cannot be said to personally know one another. Similarly, a biographer who comes to acquire large amounts of propositional knowledge about her subject does not personally know him unless at some point she has some kind of two-way personal interaction with him. The same point applies to the case of a stalker and his target. Especially interestingly, Benton notes that when someone we personally know dies, we immediately switch to the past tense when talking about our interpersonal knowledge of that person ('I *knew* her for many years') but we don't similarly switch tenses when discussing our propositional knowledge about her ('I *know that* she loved cats'). In light of a wide body of considerations, Benton proposes the following necessary conditions for interpersonal knowledge:

> S knows$_i$ R only if (i) S has had reciprocal causal contact with R, in which (ii) S treats R second-personally, and (iii) R treats S second-personally. (2017: 822)

By 'treat[ing] R second-personally,' Benton means that, 'S offers to R some of S's own thoughts, words, attitudes or emotions, and S is or for the most part intends to be attentive to R's thoughts, words, attitudes, or emotions which might be given (to S as "you") in return' (2017: 823).

I take the case made by Stump and Benton for the distinctiveness and irreducibility of interpersonal knowledge to be very compelling indeed, supported as it is by a wide and diverse body of data that are cumulatively very difficult to account for on the view that interpersonal knowledge is really just a species of propositional knowledge. In view of the case just sketched, I want to suggest that if ultimate reality is personal, then there are aspects of ultimate reality that cannot be grasped using the detached, dispassionate methods of investigation that are appropriate to the acquisition of propositional knowledge. Put another way, given the truth of theism, reality cannot be exhausted by any number of third-person descriptions. In short, it looks as though on theism the only way to gain the fullest cognitive contact with ultimate reality that we might hope to have ante-mortem is to adopt the kind of posture that is recommended by the aforementioned advocates of the involved approach: a posture that is open to a personal, two-way encounter with God. According to many theological traditions, cultivating such an openness will involve engaging in practices such as the recital of liturgy, participation in corporate worship, the appreciation of certain forms of art and music, the reading of and reflection upon scriptural narratives, and indeed, prayer. To be very clear, I am *not* saying that conditional on theism the *only* way to attain cognitive contact with ultimate reality is to step inside the praxis of some theistic religious tradition. It seems plausible to me that if theism is true then the observable world can be expected to have various features from which we can draw inferences to the existence of God. But I am suggesting that if theism is true, then our grasp of the nature of ultimate reality will be missing something crucial if we restrict ourselves exclusively to the methods of scientific and analytic philosophical inquiry which are appropriate to the acquisition of propositional knowledge about reality.

More than this, if theism is true, it seems likely that God would want humans to be able to have interpersonal knowledge both of God and of our fellow human persons. This seems especially true of those versions of theism that claim that the ultimate goal of human life is personal union with God. If God exists and does indeed wish for humans to be able to have interpersonal knowledge of God and our fellow humans, God would presumably ensure that the relevant parts of our mental architecture – perhaps especially our emotions, our moral and aesthetic sensitivities, our ability to engage in 'shared attention' (Stump, 2010: ch. 4) – were configured so as to enable us to acquire knowledge of persons in a wide range of situations. That is, given theism (or, at least, given some notable versions of theism), our cognitive and affective 'wiring' is likely to have been calibrated so as to enable us to achieve the sort of cognitive contact that is constitutive of interpersonal knowledge, including interpersonal knowledge of God.

By contrast, conditional on naturalism, given an ontological landscape on which impersonal physical entities are the explanatory and generative ground of reality, there is little reason to think that anything other than dispassionate, scientific and analytic philosophical methods of inquiry would be necessary in order to uncover the nature of ultimate reality (insofar as the nature of ultimate reality can be uncovered at all). If naturalism is true, ultimate reality ought in principle to be fully describable in purely third-person terms. The naturalist philosopher Daniel Dennett contends that, 'You've got to leave the first person out of your final theory. You won't have a theory of consciousness if you still have the first person in there, because that was what it was your job to explain' (2007: 87). More strongly, given naturalism, the methods of the involved approach are at least somewhat likely to be *misleading* in the quest for the truth about ultimate reality, coloured as they are by emotional responses that evolved for motivating survival-conducive behaviour but presumably not for giving us some special insight into the deep truths of existence.

Conditional on impersonal non-naturalistic worldviews, it is more difficult to generalise about the extent to which involved methods will be appropriate and necessary for attaining cognitive contact with ultimate reality. However, there are a couple of broad-brush points that might be made. Insofar as an impersonal non-naturalist worldview claims that consciousness is metaphysically funda-mental (the Advaita Vedanta tradition of Indian philosophy would be one such worldview), it may well be that conditional on the truth of such a worldview there are important insights into the nature of ultimate reality that are beyond the reach of scientific and analytic philosophical methods of investigation. Perhaps such insights are attainable only via involved methods, such as meditative practices that aim to bring about altered states of consciousness. In a similar vein, insofar as an impersonal non-naturalist worldview claims that moral or aesthetic value is metaphysically fundamental (for example, John Leslie's (2016) axiarchism), and insofar as emotions really can constitute veridical perceptions of value, it may be that conditional on the truth of such a worldview involved methods are required for gaining some of the most important insights into the nature of ultimate reality.

4.3 Challenges to the Involved Approach: Which Worldview to Step Inside?

The most obvious worry with the involved approach is that it seems to offer little or no guidance about how to choose *which* worldview one is to step inside. It is not as though there are just a couple of worldviews to choose from. In fact, I suggest there are two related issues here. The first is the question of how one ought to decide which worldview to inhabit in the first place. The involved approach, with its emphasis on the priority of spiritual praxis over metaphysical theorising, might seem to struggle to offer an answer to this question. The second question is this: once one has stepped inside a worldview, inhabited its praxis and ways of seeing the world, and thus opened one's heart to receiving insights that are allegedly not otherwise available, is there any way of telling whether one's venture has paid off? Is there any decisive way of telling whether one has, in fact, chosen the true worldview? Put another way, is there some discernible phenomenal quality that is present to the mind when one gains a genuine insight into reality, some quality that would be lacking if one were having a merely apparent insight? The obvious skeptical worry here is that if you had picked a different worldview to step inside, you would now be having emotionally infused experiences that *felt* just as insightful as the ones you're having within the worldview you actually chose to step inside (for a recent version of this worry, see Goldberg, 2014).

It should be noted that even if the involved approach doesn't have a clear answer to the first question, it doesn't follow that the second question lacks a good answer. In other words, suppose that the involved approach really doesn't have any helpful guidance to offer on the question of which worldview one ought to step inside in the first place. Even so, it might nevertheless be the case that there is some way of telling whether one has hit upon the truth once one has stepped inside. This might be analogous to standing in a hallway with doors leading to various rooms with no way to tell which room contains genuine gold in advance of stepping through any given door, but where the presence of genuine gold in one of the rooms is something that one can grasp after having entered that room.

John Pittard (2020: ch. 5) has recently made an extended case that there is in fact a difference in the phenomenal quality of one's experiences when one has a genuine insight into reality as compared with a merely apparent insight. The idea that there is such a thing as genuine insight – a mental state in which one grasps a non-empirical truth in an immediate, non-inferential manner and with a kind of clarity that might be expressed with the word 'Aha!' – is not uncontroversial among epistemologists (see Boghossian, 2001). Pittard contends that our ability to have epistemic access to the realms of mathematics, logic, modal metaphysics, and indeed, ethics, is cast into serious doubt if there is no such mental state (for arguments to the contrary, see Bergmann, 2021: 86–90). Pittard notes that the kinds of insight that are especially at issue when it comes to the worldview question are insights into questions of value – for example, questions about the sorts of things that it would be fitting for a supremely good being to do. Would it, for example, be fitting for a perfect being to become incarnate as a human? As regards the question of how one could know that one was having a genuine insight into such questions, Pittard draws an analogy with our knowing whilst we are awake that we are not currently dreaming:

[W]e arguably are able to discern that we are awake (when we are) because we are directly aware of the coherence and vividness of our present experience, features that we know are not characteristic of our dream experiences (even though while dreaming we may have the conviction that our experience is coherent and vivid). Similarly, when we can tell that we have genuine insight into some matter, our awareness of such insight is not achieved merely by noting that the proposition that we have such insight seems true to us. (2020: 208)

If Pittard is correct in thinking that there is such a thing as genuine insight, and that it possesses some discernible quality that is not present in cases of merely apparent insight, then perhaps there is a way to tell that one has struck gold *if* one indeed has struck gold. Pittard's analogy with waking and dreaming does, though, suggest an unsettling epistemic asymmetry: one may be able to tell as a result of having a genuine insight that one has chosen the true worldview *if* one has indeed chosen the true worldview, but if one has chosen a false worldview, one will be unable to tell in a like manner that it is false. In view of this, one might wish to look for a methodology for investigating the worldview question that doesn't suffer from such an asymmetry.

4.4 Some Varieties of the Detached Approach

The detached approach purports to offer a means for arbitrating the worldview question in a manner that allows one to avoid in any way committing to any particular worldview whilst one's investigation is still ongoing. Put another way, it claims to provide an impartial and, one might say, scientific methodology for investigating the nature of ultimate reality. The various versions of the detached approach differ from one another primarily with respect to the kind of framework that they employ for attempting to adjudicate the worldview question.

Graham Oppy (2017) favours an approach using Inference to the Best Explanation (IBE), a method which ranks theories according to how strongly they exhibit a range of explanatory virtues, especially simplicity, explanatory power, and explanatory scope. According to this framework, the best explanation of a given set of evidence is the theory that has the best overall combination of simplicity, explanatory power, and scope. Because of the fact that the IBE framework doesn't offer a way to quantify these explanatory virtues or their relative weights, inevitably there is a significant element of intuitive judgment at play in the way that theories are ranked. Whilst the IBE framework has become very popular among philosophers of science in the past few decades, the framework that has become most popular among advocates of the detached approach in the philosophy of religion is one that employs Bayes' Theorem. In what follows I shall focus on the Bayesian version of the detached approach.

Richard Swinburne (2004) and Ted Poston (2018) both advocate a Bayesian approach to aggregating the total public evidence and trying to ascertain which worldview is most strongly supported by it. There are several different (mathematically equivalent) ways to state Bayes' Theorem, but perhaps the most straightforward to grasp is the odds form:

Ratio of posteriors   Ratio of priors   Ratio of likelihoods (Bayes factor)

$$\frac{\text{Prob}(H1|E_1 \& E_2 \ldots \& E_n)}{\text{Prob}(H2|E_1 \& E_2 \ldots \& E_n)} = \frac{\text{Prob}(H1)}{\text{Prob}(H2)} \times \frac{\text{Prob}(E_1 \& E_2 \ldots \& E_n|H1)}{\text{Prob}(E_1 \& E_2 \ldots \& E_n|H2)}$$

The odds form of Bayes' Theorem supplies a formula for calculating what is known as the *ratio of posteriors*: how much more probable some hypothesis H1 is conditional on the aggregated evidence ($E_1 \& E_2 \ldots \& E_n$) than a rival hypothesis H2 is conditional on that same body of evidence. This ratio is equal to the product of two other ratios. Firstly, there is the *ratio of priors*: how much more or less probable H1 is than H2, prior to $E_1 \& E_2 \ldots \& E_n$ being taken into account. Secondly, there is the *ratio of likelihoods*, also known as the *Bayes' factor*: how much more or less likely $E_1 \& E_2 \ldots \& E_n$ is conditional on H1 than it is conditional on H2. This latter ratio is a measure of how strongly $E_1 \& E_2 \ldots \& E_n$ confirms H1 over H2.

Provided that E_1 and E_2 are two genuinely independent pieces of evidence, each of which lends support individually to H1, then the probability of H1 conditional on both pieces of evidence is greater than the probability of H1 conditional on only one of these pieces of evidence. Brandon Fitelson (2001) offers a formal definition for evidential independence, according to which two pieces of evidence E_1 and E_2 are independent of one another just in case the degree to which E_1 supports H is unaffected by whether or not E_2 is known, and the degree to which E_2 supports H is similarly unaffected by whether or not E_1 is known. Suppose that E_1 and E_2 are independent in this sense and suppose that E_1 supports H1 over H2 by a factor of 10, and that E_2 supports H1 over H2 by a factor of 10. In that case, E_1 and E_2 taken together support H1 over H2 by a factor of 100! That is, the likelihood ratios are multiplied, not added – that's the power of aggregating evidence. As Timothy McGrew and John Depoe point out, the Bayesian framework makes clear the way in which a number of individually modest or weak pieces of evidence can nevertheless amount to very powerful evidence when conjoined with one another: 'Twenty independent pieces of evidence, each of which yields a modest multiplicative ratio of 2 to 1 in favor of H when taken by itself, will combine to create a C-inductive argument with a force of more than a million to one' (2013: 307).

Let's consider a mundane example of the Bayesian framework in action. Let E_1 be the fact that upon Sally's arrival home she finds that the leaves on her front lawn are arranged in what looks like the shape of a smiley face. Let E_2 be the fact that upon Sally's arrival home she also notices what look like fresh shoe-prints on the muddy lawn. Let H1 be the hypothesis that a person went on the lawn whilst Sally was at work and let H2 be the hypothesis that nobody went on the lawn whilst she was at work. There's a lot to say about how prior probabilities are determined, but just suppose that H1 and H2 start out as equally likely prior to taking the evidence into account. The ratio of priors is thus 1/1. As for the ratio of likelihoods (or Bayes' factor), it looks plausible that the conjunction of E_1&E_2 is much more likely conditional on H1 than it is conditional on H2. Let's suppose that E_1 is 100 times more likely on H1 than on H2, and that E_2 is 100 times more likely on H1 than H2. Taken together, E_1&E_2 are 10,000 times more likely on H1 than on H2. Multiplying the ratio of priors by the ratio of likelihoods yields the result that H1 is *far* more probable than H2 on the total evidence (specifically, $1/1 \times 10,000/1 = 10,000/1$).

When it comes to the worldview question, H1 and H2 can be any pair of mutually exclusive worldviews, for example, theism and naturalism, but of course, if the two worldviews under consideration do not jointly exhaust the entire possibility space, then we will not be entitled to draw any conclusion about which worldview *overall* is most probable, but only a conclusion about the extent to which H1 is more or less probable than H2. The usual way to get H1 and H2 to exhaust the whole possibility space is to let H2 be the disjunction of all the possible worldviews that are incompatible with H1 – for example, to let H1 be theism and H2 be the disjunction of all worldviews that deny theism. The downside with doing this is that with H2 encompassing so many different worldviews, it gets considerably harder to try to estimate the likelihood of any given piece of evidence conditional on H2. Paul Draper (2010: 420) complains that in practice it is very often theism and naturalism that are compared, with little thought given to the non-naturalistic alternatives to theism.

Some advocates of the Bayesian approach favour trying to plug in fairly specific numerical values into the Bayesian formula, whilst others take a more circumspect approach to the numbers. Ted Poston (2018) offers perhaps the most developed proposal for how to try to assign numerical values. He proposes using a logarithmic scale with base-10, that is, powers of 10. Thus, for a given bit of evidence E, a logarithmic likelihood ratio (LLR) of 1 in favour of H1 means that E supports H1 over H2 by a Bayes' factor of 10. An LLR of 2 in favour of H1 means that E supports H1 over H2 by a Bayes' factor of 100. An LLR of 3 in favour of H1 means that E supports H1 over H2 by a Bayes' factor of 1,000, and so on. As Poston writes, 'An attractive feature of using logarithms is that it turns multiplication into addition' (2018: 379). In other words, if E_1 has an LLR of 1 in favour of H1 and E_2 has an LLR of 3 in favour of H1, their combined LLR is 4 (= a Bayes' factor of 10,000). Poston suggests that we can gain a helpful sense of how strong a given Bayes' factor really is by considering statistician Richard Royall's (1997: 12) illustration involving two hypotheses about the contents of an urn from which someone is drawing and replacing balls, one at a time: the first hypothesis says that the urn contains only white balls, while the second hypothesis says that the urn contains half white balls and half black balls. Consider the strength of evidence for the all-white-urn hypothesis that is provided by a given number n of successive white balls being drawn from the urn. Three successive white draws seems intuitively like quite strong evidence that the urn contains only white balls, while 20 successive white draws seems intuitively like overwhelming evidence that the urn contains only white balls. The Bayes' factors and LLRs can be precisely calculated in an example like this. So, three white draws yields a Bayes' factor of 8 in favour of the all-white-urn hypothesis, which is an LLR of roughly .9, while 20 successive white draws yields a Bayes' factor of 1,048,576 in favour of the all-white-urn hypothesis, which is an LLR of slightly over 6. Poston suggests that for each independent argument in favour of a given worldview, we can assign an LLR of 1 in favour of the worldview in question. If there were six independent arguments for theism and four independent arguments for naturalism, that would yield an LLR of 6/4 = 1.5 in favour of theism.

Swinburne (2004) also ventures some numerical values. For example, he suggests that the probability of the total public evidence conditional on theism is roughly 1/3 and he gestures at a much lower, though unspecified, probability for the total public evidence conditional on naturalism. He is often quoted out of context on this matter, however, and in fact he is keen to emphasise that such numerical values shouldn't be taken very literally: 'I stress again that it is impossible to give anything like exact numerical values to the probabilities involved in these calculations. I have attempted to bring out the force of my arguments by giving some arbitrary values that do, I hope, capture within the roughest of ranges the kinds of probabilities involved' (2004: 341).

Perhaps the biggest advantage of the Bayesian version of the detached approach is that it offers a transparent methodology for aggregating together lots of smaller sub-judgments about probabilities into a single overall judgment. This is important for at least two reasons. Firstly, humans are prone to commit probabilistic fallacies (such as the base rate fallacy) when attempting to make complex probability judgments in an undisciplined way, and the Bayesian framework helps us to avoid these. Secondly, it is easier to achieve a measure of cross-worldview consensus with respect to the smaller sub-judgments than with respect to overall probability judgments. Some theists, for example, are willing to grant that evil is pretty improbable given theism (Benton, Hawthorne, & Isaacs, 2016); some non-theists are willing to grant that fine-tuning is pretty improbable given naturalism (Draper, 2002: 199–200).

Another benefit is that the Bayesian framework can enable us to see how low a prior probability for a given worldview someone would need to have in order rationally to reject that worldview in light of evidence favouring that worldview by a Bayes' factor of n. Suppose that Bob accepts that fine-tuning favours theism over the disjunction of non-theistic worldviews by a Bayes' factor of at least 1,000 (an LLR of 3). If this were Bob's only evidence concerning theism, then in order to rationally reject theism it would need to be rational for Bob to assign a prior probability to theism of less than 1/1000.

4.5 Challenges to the Detached Approach: Not So Detached after All?

At the end of the day, formal frameworks still require raw material as input, in the form of judgments about how likely E is given H and how likely it is given ¬H, and about how intrinsically likely H is. When we are dealing with mundane matters such as the likelihood of someone having a tertiary education conditional on their living in a certain postal code, we can try to align our probability estimates with statistical frequencies. By contrast, many of the probabilities that are at issue in the worldview debate cannot be determined by appeal to statistical frequencies, where I have in mind things like the probability of there existing embodied conscious agents conditional on naturalism, or the probability that the God of classical theism would become incarnate. Somewhere in between would be those matters upon which statistical frequencies have some bearing but are perhaps not entirely sufficient to determine the relevant probabilities. An example might be the probability that the New Testament gospels would accurately preserve many obscure details about first-century Palestinian topography, landmarks, personal names, epithets, and complicated regional political arrangements conditional on the gospels' having been the end result of a process of testimonial transmission resembling the telephone game at children's parties.

To be clear, I am not at all claiming that the only genuine probabilities are statistical frequencies. Nor am I saying that we cannot sensibly offer reasons on behalf of our probability estimates for propositions that have metaphysical import. The point is simply that it is much more difficult to see how to assign numerical values to things like the probability of the existence of embodied consciousness conditional on naturalism or the probability that the God of classical theism would become incarnate. Intuitive judgments unavoidably come into play in attempting to discern such probabilities. The worry, then, is that no matter how impartial the mechanism of aggregating the various sub-units is, the end result is still going to be coloured by the way in which our pre-existing commitments have influenced the intuitive judgments that served as the inputs. It is sometimes observed, moreover, that in practice this procedure invariably does yield the very result to which an author was already committed. Robert McKim articulates the concern as follows:

> [A]ttempts to quantify the evidence seem very dubious. They have a remarkable tendency to yield results that confirm what was already believed. One wonders, for example, how often the relevant calculation has resulted in a previously held religious position being rejected ... It is obvious that for every Richard Swinburne who adds up what he thinks to be the relevant evidence and gets a result that supports theism, there is a J. L. Mackie who gets an entirely different result. (2001: 22, 24)

Two further points of concern might be noted. Firstly, in view of the difficulty of assigning numerical probabilities with any precision, something Swinburne (2004: 341) readily admits, there is a worry about the way that margins for error accumulate when we are aggregating lots of such probabilities. Our probability judgments about such things as the likelihood of embodied consciousness given naturalism or the likelihood of an incarnation given theism are in reality no more fine-grained than what is expressed by phrases such as 'very likely,' 'overwhelmingly unlikely,' 'a bit more likely than not,' and so on. But each of these locutions corresponds to wide ranges of numerical values. The margins for error are considerable. This only gets amplified when lots of individual values with wide margins for error are multiplied together.

Secondly, there is some empirical data that suggests that 'insight' approaches to problem-solving are more accurate than 'analytical' approaches (Salvi et al., 2016). Roughly, analytical approaches are those that involve the attempt to use some kind of step-wise methodology – for example, trying to solve an anagram by way of some method such as swapping letters 1 and 2, then swapping letters 1 and 3, then swapping letters 1 and 4, and so on, until one finds what looks like a solution. Roughly, insight approaches involve not attempting to use any such step-wise methodology but instead attempting simply to hold the problem or datum at the centre of one's attention and wait until a solution springs to mind. Admittedly, given that these studies concern people's ability to find correct solutions to puzzles, anagrams, word association games, and the like, it is not straightforward to work out whether the findings are strongly relevant to the question of how to investigate the nature of ultimate reality. But it is at least worth keeping in mind.

4.6 Holistic Judgments and the Weighing of the Total Evidence

A third way, which in some sense synthesises elements of the involved and detached approaches, might be to maintain that making a serious effort at weighing the total public evidence is necessary for arriving at a rational view on the question of the nature of ultimate reality, and yet, to insist that such a weighing process can legitimately involve – indeed, that it is psychologically impossible for it not to involve – emotionally infused, impressionistic judgments that only emerge when one beholds the evidential landscape in its totality. Such an approach has been gestured at by John Henry Newman (1872), Basil Mitchell (1973), and William Abraham (1987). Indeed, Paul Draper (2010: 422–3) seems to be thinking along these lines in suggesting that when one steps back from the details and surveys the whole range of striking phenomena – consciousness, morality, free will, cosmic fine-tuning, religious experience, and the rest – it may be more plausible to take them at face value rather than to regard them all as being illusory, even if each item taken on its own can be satisfactorily explained away in naturalistic terms.

The sort of holistic judgment I have in mind is akin to the impression one has when beholding a painting in its totality. Whatever that feeling is, it isn't simply the result of aggregating the feelings that one has about each of the sub-units of the painting that would result from dividing it into sixty-four squares, for example. But, of course, the impressionistic judgment about the totality is *informed by* one's judgments about those sub-units. Hence, this approach isn't by any means eschewing the idea that trying to get clearer about the evidential force of individual items of evidence is very important. The Bayesian framework can be very useful at a local level, then. Indeed, many philosophers who employ Bayes' Theorem do not attempt to assign precise numerical values, but instead see the value of Bayes' Theorem as residing in the way that it provides such clarity about the relationship between the various sub-judgments. My claim, then, is just that an attempt to use such a formal framework to calculate the overall force of the total evidence is beset with problems pertaining to the numerical imprecision of our sub-judgments and their propensity to be coloured by our overarching impressions of the landscape. Put another way, we are probably kidding ourselves that what we are engaged in is a dispassionate calculation of the combined force of all the items that make up the public evidence. It is better to be realistic about the fact that we are guided in no small part by emotionally infused, perhaps even aesthetically sensitive, judgments about the total landscape. W. V. O. Quine perhaps recognised this point when he remarked of his austere naturalist, nominalist worldview that he had 'a taste for desert landscapes' (1953: 4).

The obvious drawback of this approach is that it doesn't afford a high degree of precision in making the case for one's favoured conclusion about the world-view question. It can seem, moreover, particularly to those with a left-brained sensibility, to be unacceptably idiosyncratic or subjective. But as William Abraham notes, even the hard sciences involve the making of judgments that cannot always be reduced to an algorithm. As he puts it, 'Personal judgment simply means the ability to weigh evidence without using some sort of formal calculus. No one can ever have an excess of such ability' (1987: 34). The advantage of this approach is that whilst taking account of the importance of grappling with the evidence to the best of our abilities, it does so in a way that is realistic about human psychology.

5 Evidential Ambiguity as Evidence in Its Own Right

Evidential ambiguity can have epistemic significance in two quite distinct ways. On the one hand, a situation's being evidentially ambiguous makes it more challenging to get at the truth of the matter in question. Sections 2, 3, and 4 have been exploring the contours of this challenge as it pertains to the question of which worldview is true. On the other hand, that a situation is evidentially ambiguous can *itself* be evidence for or against certain hypotheses, to the degree that an evidentially ambiguous situation is more what we would expect to find on some hypotheses than on others. This final section is going to consider the degree to which the evidential ambiguity that we encounter with respect to the worldview question might actually be evidence in favour of some worldviews over against others.

5.1 Evidential Ambiguity as Disambiguating

Before we go any further, let's briefly consider a mundane example of how evidential ambiguity could itself be evidence that favours one hypothesis over its rivals. Imagine that the guitarist of a famous rock band disappears in mysterious circumstances: his car is found abandoned on a bridge with a steep drop over a deep and wide river, but his body is never found, there is no suicide note, and there were no prior hints to friends or family of anything untoward. As such, the evidence is ambiguous as regards the question of his fate. Did he commit suicide? Or did he perhaps run away to start a new life in secret away from the spotlight? The situation is perplexing. Let's suppose, though, that we know that the musician's personality was such that if he was going to commit suicide, then he would have wanted his fans to know why, but that if he had intended to run away and start a new life in secret, he would have wanted the evidence to be murky and inconclusive so as to create intrigue about his fate and so that he couldn't easily be traced. As such, the ambiguity of the evidence is actually more strongly predicted by the hypothesis that he ran away than by the hypothesis that he committed suicide. This is a case in which evidential ambiguity is itself evidence that supports one particular hypothesis over its rivals.

Is this how things are with the worldview question? Is the evidential ambiguity of the public evidence itself evidence that supports some worldviews over others? J. L. Schellenberg (2015) has argued that theism strongly predicts – indeed, *entails* – that there would not be any evidential ambiguity about whether God exists, in view of the way that a loving God would want every non-resistant human person to have the opportunity for relationship with God at every waking moment and given that having such relationship requires that a person believes that God exists. As such, according to Schellenberg, evidential ambiguity is strong – indeed, *decisive* – evidence against theism:

> Any apparent inconclusiveness in the evidence must … *itself* be taken as a consideration (evidentially) justifying the conclusion that God does not exist. (1993: 212, emphasis original)

> If there was good reason for God to prevent religious ambiguity, then this very evidential situation might be *dis*ambiguating, showing that all things considered – that is, with the fact of ambiguity included in the evidence – the world *wasn't* religiously ambiguous but instead spoke clearly against the existence of God. (2015: 37, emphasis original)

The agnostic philosopher of religion Paul Draper has suggested a reason that the theist might offer for thinking things are actually the other way round, in other words, that evidential ambiguity is more to be expected on theism than on naturalism: 'A theist might counter that ambiguous evidence, as opposed to strong evidence against theism, is actually evidence for theism, because ambiguity is more likely when someone controls what evidence is available, and such control is entailed by theism but not by naturalism' (2002: 209).

Whether or not there is merit to this suggestion about someone controlling what evidence is available, Draper's framing of the issues here is implicitly being done in terms of a Bayesian likelihoods ratio (we encountered the notion of a likelihoods ratio in §4.4). He is in effect asking: How likely is evidential ambiguity conditional on theism as compared with how likely evidential ambiguity is conditional on naturalism? This runs parallel to the way in which most philosophers who discuss the problem of evil tend to frame that issue nowadays. That is, rather than frame the issue in terms of the idea that God's existence is logically incompatible with the occurrence of evil, it is far more common nowadays to frame the issue in terms of the existence of certain kinds of evils or the amount or distribution of evil in the world as being strong evidence against theism, in virtue of these things being allegedly much more likely on non-theistic worldviews than on theism (see Benton, Hawthorne, & Isaacs, 2016: 1). William Rowe, an atheist and advocate of probabilistic versions of the problem of evil, wrote in 1979 that, 'Some philosophers have contended that the existence of evil is logically inconsistent with the existence of the theistic God. No one, I think, has succeeded in establishing such an extravagant claim' (1979: 335n1). Very few philosophers have subsequently attempted to formulate the problem of evil in terms of an alleged logical incompatibility. Put simply, showing that a hypothesis H is logically incompatible with some fact E is a far harder task than showing that E is less probable on H than on ¬H. In order to refute the claim that God is logically incompatible with E, someone only needs to show that there is some logically possible world in which God and E co-exist (Plantinga, 1974: ch. 9) – such a possible world need not closely resemble the actual world – whereas in order to show that E is not strong evidence against the existence of God, someone would need to show that theism actually makes E nearly as probable as non-theistic worldviews do.

Schellenberg continues to favour a deductive formulation of the argument from divine hiddenness that uses a premise alleging that God's existence is logically incompatible with there being any evidential ambiguity about God's existence. Due to the dominance of Schellenberg's deductive formulation in the hiddenness literature and the way in which subsequent contributors have mostly adopted his deductive framing of the issues (see, e.g., Howard-Snyder & Moser, 2002; Stump & Green, 2015), there has been an almost exclusive focus in the hiddenness literature on the question of whether theism is logically compatible with evidential ambiguity, to the neglect of the question of whether we would expect evidential ambiguity given naturalism or other non-theistic worldviews. Draper's Bayesian likelihoods framing allows us to see that the latter question is just as important as the question of how strongly we should expect evidential ambiguity on theism. A few philosophers of religion from various sides of the worldview debate have begun to frame the hiddenness problem in probabilistic terms akin to Draper's formulation, notably Stephen Maitzen (2006), Jason Marsh (2013), Charity Anderson (2017, 2021), and Matthew Braddock (2023). I too shall adopt this probabilistic way of framing the issues in what follows.

5.2 What Are the Evidential Ambiguity Facts?

What we are trying to do, then, is to ascertain whether evidential ambiguity adds anything as evidence for or against a given worldview *once all of the other evidence has been taken into account*. That is, suppose that the evidential force of the various natural theological data (fine-tuning, consciousness, morality, reports of religious experiences, and all the rest of it) and the data about evil and suffering in the world have already been taken into account: what other facts are left over that might plausibly constitute the evidence from evidential ambiguity itself? Well, there are those characterisations of evidential ambiguity we explored in Section 3, some of which I suggested were both interesting (in the sense of not just applying to the vast majority of our beliefs about the world) and worldview-neutral (in the sense of not presupposing or privileging any particular worldview), namely:

(i) that the body of facts that comprises the public evidence is extremely large and complex and spans numerous areas of expertise;

(ii) that the total public evidence has the property of being mixed, in the sense that it contains at least one subset that, when taken in isolation, fairly strongly supports one particular worldview (or family of worldviews), and at least one other subset that, when taken in isolation, fairly strongly supports a rival worldview (or rival family of worldviews).

I also suggested at the beginning of Section 4 that a further way of characterising evidential ambiguity might be that it is difficult for us to work out how to go about investigating the question at hand, and I suggested that that may well be rooted in something that was observed in §2.5, namely:

(iii) that the answer to the question of what are the smallest changes to our epistemic situation (i.e., our cognitive abilities, our vantage point, the facts of the matter) that would be needed in order to render our situation with respect to the worldview question wholly unambiguous will be different conditional on the truth of different worldviews.

In addition, the following facts might also be seen as part of the evidential ambiguity facts:

(iv) facts about the contents of human worldview beliefs, including demographic facts about percentages of humans who hold a given worldview and their distribution throughout space and time;

(v) as per the account of the threefold sources of evidential ambiguity in §2.4, facts about the kinds of cognitive abilities human beings have.

Plausibly, some of these facts explain others of these facts. For example, the fact that humans have diverse and mutually incompatible worldview beliefs is explained at least in part by the fact that the public evidence is mixed and the fact that it's very complex. The fact that the evidence that is available to us is mixed is in part explained by the kinds of cognitive abilities we have (as outlined in §2.4). But it is very difficult to disentangle the dependence relationships among these different facts; it is very difficult to figure out how much of a causal contribution some of these facts make to bringing about others of these facts. As such, I won't attempt here to disentangle them but will just treat them as a family of facts that need to be dealt with holistically.

5.3 Isolating the Evidential Contribution of Evidential Ambiguity

What we need to do is to try to isolate the evidential significance of the evidential ambiguity facts in order to ascertain what contribution (if any) they make *over and above* the natural theological evidence and the evidence from evil. Why is it important to try to isolate their evidential contribution in this way? Well, just suppose for the sake of argument that a complex, life-supporting universe is far more probable on theism than on naturalism. A complex, life-supporting universe is a precondition for there to be evidential ambiguity regarding the worldview question – recall that in §2.3 we saw that evidential ambiguity is always evidential ambiguity *for some finite agent(s)*. Given that that which is a necessary precondition for an evidentially ambiguous situation to exist in the first place (namely, fine-tuning) is far more probable on theism than on naturalism, one might be tempted to conclude that evidential ambiguity itself is therefore far more probable on theism than on naturalism, and hence that evidential ambiguity strongly supports theism over naturalism. But that would be a mistaken way of framing the issues.

In general, from the fact that X is a necessary precondition for Y, together with the fact X supports a hypothesis H1 over its rival hypothesis H2, we can't conclude *anything* about what evidential significance Y may have over and above X's evidential significance. A mundane example illustrates this. Suppose that new neighbours have just moved in next door to you. They leave you a wrapped gift on your doorstep (call this fact GIFT). Let's suppose that GIFT is substantially more probable on the hypothesis that the new neighbours want to be friends with you (call this hypothesis FRIENDS) than on the hypothesis that they don't want to be friends with you (call this hypothesis NOT FRIENDS). Suppose, further, that when you remove the wrapping paper, what you find inside is an already opened and partially consumed bottle of very cheap wine (call this fact BAD GIFT). Clearly, GIFT is a necessary precondition for BAD GIFT. But equally clearly, from the fact that GIFT supports FRIENDS over NOT FRIENDS, it does *not* follow that BAD GIFT also supports FRIENDS over NOT FRIENDS. Hence why it is so important to isolate the evidential contribution of BAD GIFT from the evidential contribution of GIFT.

In order to isolate the evidential contribution that BAD GIFT makes from the evidential contribution that GIFT makes, what we need to do is consider the likelihood of BAD GIFT given that the neighbours want to be friends *and* given that they've left you a gift (i.e., the likelihood of BAD GIFT conditional on FRIENDS & GIFT), and compare this with the likelihood of BAD GIFT given that the neighbours don't want to be friends *and* given that they've left you a gift (i.e., the likelihood of BAD GIFT conditional on NOT FRIENDS & GIFT). In other words, we're now taking GIFT as a given – reflecting the fact that we've already taken its evidential contribution into account – and we're asking how strongly each of the hypotheses, when conjoined with GIFT, predicts a more specific fact about the situation: namely, BAD GIFT. Plausibly, BAD GIFT is quite a lot more likely on NOT FRIENDS & GIFT than it is on FRIENDS & GIFT.

Figure 1 uses Bayesian bars to illustrate how this works, where each bar represents your total probability space at different stages of the situation (for more on Bayesian bars, see Hawthorne, 2013; Page, 2020):

(a) FRIENDS and NOT FRIENDS start out equally probable; the conditional prior probability of GIFT given FRIENDS is half; the conditional prior probability of GIFT given NOT FRIENDS is a quarter.

(b) After you have conditionalised on GIFT (i.e., taken GIFT into account by eliminating all the NO GIFT portions of the probability space), FRIENDS becomes twice as probable as NOT FRIENDS.

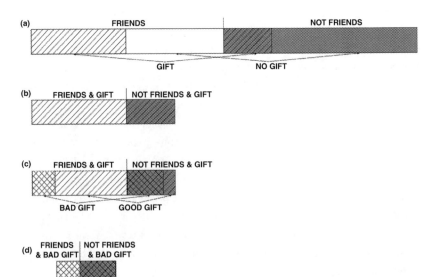

Figure 1 Bayesian bars

(c) The evidential force of GIFT has been taken into account, and we are now interested in different ways that GIFT could be true: namely, BAD GIFT and GOOD GIFT. BAD GIFT is unlikely conditional on FRIENDS; whereas BAD GIFT is quite likely conditional on NOT FRIENDS.

(d) After you have conditionalised on BAD GIFT (i.e., taken BAD GIFT into account by eliminating all the GOOD GIFT portions of the probability space), NOT FRIENDS becomes somewhat more probable than FRIENDS.

This example illustrates why it is crucial that we isolate the evidential contribution that evidential ambiguity itself makes from the evidential contribution that other items of evidence make (including items of evidence that may be a precondition for there to be an evidentially ambiguous situation in the first place, such as the fine-tuning of the universe). As with the example just discussed, what we need to do is ask how likely the evidential ambiguity facts are, given the truth of a particular worldview *and* given the natural theological facts and the facts of evil (sometimes I'll refer to the totality of the natural theological facts and the facts of evil as *the primary facts* for the sake of ease).

For example, even supposing for the sake of argument that naturalism makes the primary facts very unlikely overall, we're going to bracket that point and ask how likely evidential ambiguity is in a godless world which is ultimately composed entirely of physical entities and which is fine-tuned, contains life, including complex conscious life, reports of religious experiences, contains evil of the kinds and amounts found in our world, and all the rest of it. As the foregoing example about the neighbours' gift illustrated, it is irrelevant for our present purposes to allege that some aspect of the primary facts that is a precondition for evidential ambiguity (for instance, fine-tuning) is very improbable on naturalism. Or, switching our focus from the probability of evidential ambiguity on naturalism to the probability of evidential ambiguity on theism, even supposing for the sake of the argument that theism makes the primary facts very unlikely overall, we're going to bracket that point and ask how likely evidential ambiguity is in a world which is created by a God with the traditional attributes and which is fine-tuned, contains life, including complex conscious life, reports of religious experiences, contains evil of the kinds and amounts found in our world, and all the rest of it. Again, as the neighbours' gift example illustrates, it is irrelevant for our present purposes to allege that some aspects of the primary facts that heavily contribute to the evidential ambiguity of our situation (the facts of evil, perhaps) are themselves very improbable on theism.

In short, for the purposes of assessing the distinctive evidential contribution of evidential ambiguity, we must ask how likely an evidentially ambiguous situation is, given the truth of a particular worldview *and* given the existence of the primary facts (fine-tuning, complex life, consciousness, reports of religious experience, the amounts and kinds of evil that occur in our world, and so on). Only by approaching the question in this way will we be in a position to try to assess whether evidential ambiguity itself adds anything distinctive to the case for or against theism or adds anything distinctive to the case for or against naturalism, or indeed, adds anything distinctive to the case for or against any impersonal non-naturalist worldview.

5.4 Why Evidential Ambiguity Is Likely, Given Naturalism-Plus-the-Primary-Facts

What I want to suggest now is that in a world in which naturalism is true and in which there is fine-tuning, embodied life including beings with complex self-awareness, reports of religious experiences, and the kinds of evils that occur in our world, it is highly likely that finite, embodied creatures like us would encounter evidential ambiguity with respect to the worldview question. Here are three reasons for supposing this to be the case.

Firstly, other things being equal, the larger and more complex a set of evidence is, the more scope there is for some subsets of that evidence to be misleading (that is, to point to a false conclusion if taken in isolation), and hence, the more scope there is for the total evidence to be mixed. Any universe in which there is fine-tuning, embodied life, beings with complex self-awareness, reports of religious experiences, and the sorts of evils that occur in our world, is going to be a universe in which the public evidence pertaining to the worldview question is very extensive and complex, owing to the sheer number of distinct items of relevant evidence that exist and the vast web of causal and explanatory interrelationships between them.

Secondly, any undesigned universe that has all the features that are needed for the emergence of life is very probably going to *appear* to be designed, despite not actually being so. Such apparently designed features, in conjunction with the facts of evil, will tend to yield a set of public evidence that is mixed as regards the worldview question.

Thirdly, in an undesigned universe that gives rise to intelligent living beings, there exists no superintending designer to ensure alignment between the kinds of cognitive faculties possessed by those intelligent beings and the deep truths of reality. For instance, in such a universe there is no reason to expect that such beings would evolve to have cognitive faculties that enable them to have straightforward access to the truth of propositions such as that *all that exists is ultimately composed entirely of physical entities* or that *death results in the permanent cessation of conscious experience*. Hence, it won't be too surprising if the evidence that is accessible to intelligent beings in a universe of the sort we're considering is such as to leave them perplexed.

These points apply not just to naturalistic worldviews but to any worldview that doesn't postulate intelligent agency as the explanatory and generative ground floor of reality, or at any rate, any worldview that doesn't claim that ultimate reality has purposes that include the flourishing of sentient creatures.

5.5 Why Evidential Ambiguity Is Likely, Given Theism-Plus-the-Primary-Facts

I want to suggest that in a world in which theism is true and in which there is fine-tuning, embodied life including beings with complex self awareness, reports of religious experiences, the kinds of evils that occur in our world, and so on, it is highly likely that finite, embodied creatures like us would encounter evidential ambiguity with respect to the worldview question. None of the following points assume that evidential ambiguity is a species of evil or that the problem of evidential ambiguity is a subset of the problem of evil – I don't think it is. But for the following reasons, an evidentially ambiguous situation seems to me to be very probable on theism if there are good reasons for God to permit the facts of evil, as there must be if both theism and the facts of evil are the case. Again, in order to ascertain whether evidential ambiguity adds any-thing to the case against theism over and above what the facts of evil contribute, we need to think about how likely evidential ambiguity would be in a world where both God and evil of the kinds found in our world exist. I shall outline three reasons for thinking that evidential ambiguity would be very likely in any world of that sort.

Firstly, the facts of evil are very plausibly the most powerful piece of counterevidence against theism. Hence, all else being equal, the total public evidence would point much more clearly towards theism were it not for the facts of evil. Arguably the total public evidence would no longer be mixed (in the sense outlined in §3.5) were the existence of evil to be erased from the world. In short, a mixed set of evidence is virtually entailed by the conjunction of theism and the facts of evil. Relatedly, the facts of evil are among the leading causes of non-belief among humans, if not *the* leading cause; without the facts of evil there would be far less non-belief than there is (and note that the facts about the prevalence of non-belief might well be included among the evidential ambigu-ity facts, as outlined in §5.2). I take it that it would have been within God's power to have counteracted the evidence from evil more strongly by providing more numerous and more powerful religious experiences, but that leads me onto the second point.

Secondly, conditional on theism and on God's having good reasons to permit the facts of evil (again, as we're currently assuming for the sake of isolating the evidential contribution of evidential ambiguity), it is not unlikely that God's reasons for permitting evil would include the value of soul-making: the cultivation of virtues of moral character such as courage, patience, endurance, kindness, and generosity in the face of adversity, scarcity, and danger. Theodicies that appeal to the value of soul-making are among the most prominent theodicies in the history of philosophy (Hick, 1979), and it would be somewhat surprising if God's actual reasons for permitting evil bore no resemblance at all to the various possible reasons suggested by philosophers of religion over the centuries. Importantly, it has been argued by some theodicists that an arena in which soul-making can take place requires there to be substantial 'epistemic distance' between God and humans – or in other words, a substantial amount of evidential ambiguity regarding God's existence. John Hick argues that the soul-making function of suffering would be undermined if everyone was at all times sure that there exists a God who has a good reason for permitting every instance of terrible suffering; 'dysteleological' (i.e., apparently pointless) suffering is a necessary feature of a vale of soul-making. As he puts it,

> It seems, then, that in a world that is to be the scene of compassionate love and self-giving for others, suffering must fall upon mankind with something of the haphazardness and inequity that we now experience. It must be apparently unmerited, pointless, and incapable of being morally rationalised. For it is precisely this feature of our common human lot that creates sympathy between man and man and evokes the unselfishness, kindness and goodwill which are among the highest values of personal life. (1979: 370–71)

The appearance of pointlessness cannot obtain in a world in which God's existence is abundantly obvious for all to see. In short, it is not unlikely that God's reasons for permitting the facts of evil would include God's desire to realise certain higher-order goods that cannot come into existence unless there is a significant degree of evidential ambiguity regarding God's existence.

Thirdly, conditional on God's existing and having good reasons to permit the facts of evil (again, as we're assuming for the purpose of isolating the evidential contribution of evidential ambiguity), it is not unlikely that God's reasons for permitting evil would include God's desire for humans to exercise a robust kind of freedom, one which involves our being the sorts of creatures who can bless or harm one another in serious ways (Swinburne, 1998). Theodicies that invoke human freedom are among the most prominent theodicies in the history of philosophy, and again, it would be somewhat surprising if God's actual reasons for permitting evil bore no resemblance whatsoever to the various possible reasons put forward by philosophers of religion over the centuries. If God's permission of evil is indeed partly due to God's desire for humans to exercise the aforementioned kind of robust freedom, there are at least two things that flow from this, both of which are relevant to the likelihood of there being an evidentially ambiguous situation.

For one thing, as Richard Swinburne (2004: chs. 10–11) has argued at some length and I have developed further (Baker-Hytch, 2016: 379–85), our having a robust kind of freedom and responsibility for one another's well-being requires our having bodies that instantiate a delicate balance of powers, limitations, and vulnerabilities, including a delicate balance of cognitive powers and limitations. As I argued in §2.4, one key determinant of the extent to which a situation is evidentially ambiguous for an agent S is the kinds of cognitive abilities S has. The cognitive limitations that are part of the delicate balance needed for humans to exercise a robust kind of freedom and responsibility for one another's well-being will have a bearing on our ability to access facts that are relevant to the worldview question, and hence will make our situation more evidentially ambiguous than it would have been if we'd had (say) angel-like cognitive abilities. Here are a couple of examples of cognitive limitations that it might be argued God would need humans to have if we are to have a significant degree of mutual responsibility for one another's well-being: (i) not being able to literally read the minds of others, given the way that privacy over one's own thoughts is arguably essential to being able to form long-range plans that pertain to the well-being of others; (ii) not having the ability to perceive in an unmediated way events that are occurring far outside of one's immediate location in space and time, given the way that the ability to form complex plans and carry them out arguably requires that other humans not be able to perceive one's every move from afar.

Another point related to the value of humans exercising robust freedom is as follows. A species of creatures who have something like the balance of cognitive powers and limitations that humans do will be mutually dependent on one another not just for acquiring material goods (food, shelter, and so on), but also for acquiring intellectual goods (justified belief, knowledge, understanding). This in turn means that such creatures will have significant scope to be influenced by one another intellectually. Short of God intervening miraculously every time someone forms the intention to influence another person's religious beliefs away from theism, these creatures will have it within their power to give one another defeaters for belief in God and to influence one another to adopt non-theistic worldview beliefs. Were God to have a consistent policy of stepping in to defeat every defeater that anyone ever acquired for theism, that would be severely freedom-curtailing. Indeed, Charity Anderson has plausibly suggested that if God were to adopt a policy of defeating every defeater for theism that any person ever encounters, that would very likely require God to provide 'fireworks or something similarly overwhelming' (2017: 128). Accordingly, the actual-world facts about the tremendous diversity of different kinds of worldview beliefs (which I suggested in §5.2 might be seen to be part of the evidential ambiguity facts) would not be overly surprising if God exists and wishes humans to exercise the aforementioned sort of robust freedom and responsibility for one another's well-being.

5.6 Concluding Thoughts

Drawing these threads together, what I have suggested is that in a world in which God exists and permits evils of the kinds found in our world to occur, it is very likely that finite, embodied creatures like us would encounter a substantial degree of evidential ambiguity regarding God's existence. There are two sorts of reasons for this. For one thing, evil itself – at least on the face of it – is strong evidence against the existence of God, and so the existence of substantial amounts of evil alongside the various positive evidences for theism (fine-tuning, consciousness, reports of religious experiences, and so on) yields a mixed set of evidence. For another thing, for God to co-exist alongside substantial amounts of evil it must be the case that God has good reasons for permitting such evil, and insofar as those reasons include the value of soul-making and the value of robust creaturely freedom (as the two most prominent kinds of theodicies contend they do), then that is a further reason to expect evidential ambiguity. This is because a soul-making arena plausibly requires God's existence to be veiled from us to a significant degree, and because the delicate balance of cognitive powers and limitations that we would need to have in order to have a robust kind of freedom and mutual responsibility for one another's well-being would be such as to place significant limits on our epistemic access to the world and to make us liable to acquire defeaters from one another for our religious beliefs. In short, if it is true that evidential ambiguity is not what one would expect to find, given theism, that will be because various facts that contribute heavily to the evidential ambiguity of our situation – especially facts having to do with the kinds of evil our world contains – are themselves improbable on theism; evidential ambiguity itself adds very little over and above those facts.

I also suggested that in a world in which naturalism is true and in which there is fine-tuning, complex life, beings with sophisticated consciousness, reports of religious experience, the sorts of evil that we find in our world, and so on, it is very likely that finite, embodied creatures like us would encounter evidential ambiguity with respect to the worldview question. In short, this is because an undesigned world with all these remarkable features will have to be very complex, it will contain many features that will *appear* designed, and the intelligent creatures who inhabit it will possess cognitive faculties that have not been intentionally designed to give them deep insights into the mysteries of the universe. These points also seem to apply to any impersonal non-naturalist worldview on which ultimate reality doesn't have purposes that include the flourishing of intelligent creatures.

In sum, when we properly separate out the contribution of evidential ambiguity from the contribution of what I have called 'the primary facts' – that is, all the usual evidences cited for and against the major worldviews *other than* the facts of evidential ambiguity – we find that the evidential contribution of evidential ambiguity itself is minimal. Evidential ambiguity is very likely on naturalism-plus-the-primary-facts, it is very likely on some forms of impersonal non-naturalism-plus-the-primary-facts, and it is very likely on theism-plus-the-primary-facts. The upshot of all this is that evidential ambiguity itself adds very little in terms of evidence for or against any of the major worldviews.

There is one final thought I would like to offer. Throughout this Element, the ambiguity that has been in view pertains to what I have called 'the public evidence', which I defined in §2.3 as the body of public facts that are in principle accessible via the sorts of ordinary cognitive abilities that virtually all humans would recognise as real. Or put another way, the public evidence is that body of facts that can be known through detached human methods of inquiry. As I suggested in Section 4, if ultimate reality is personal, then there is reason to think that there are aspects of it that are inaccessible to such detached methods of investigation. Hence, on theism, the public evidence is not the whole picture; indeed, the public evidence is very far from being the whole picture. Given theism, then, it shouldn't be surprising that the rather incomplete picture afforded to us by the public evidence is less than fully decisive.

References

Abraham, W. J. (1987). Cumulative Case Arguments for Christian Theism. In W. J. Abraham & S. W. Holtzer, eds., *The Rationality of Religious Belief: Essays in Honour of Basil Mitchell*. Oxford: Oxford University Press, 17–37.

Allison, D. C. (2022). *Encountering Mystery: Religious Experience in a Secular Age*. Grand Rapids, MI: Eerdmans Publishing Co.

Alston, W. P. (1991). *Perceiving God: The Epistemology of Religious Experience*. Ithaca, NY: Cornell University Press.

Anderson, C. (2017). Divine Hiddenness: Defeated Evidence. *Royal Institute of Philosophy Supplement*, **81**, 119–32.

(2021). Divine Hiddenness: An Evidential Argument. *Philosophical Perspectives*, **35**, 5–22.

Baker-Hytch, M. (2016). Mutual Epistemic Dependence and the Demographic Divine Hiddenness Problem. *Religious Studies*, **52**(3), 375–94.

(2023). Natural Theology and Religious Belief. In J. Fuqua, J. Greco, & T. McNab, eds., *The Cambridge Handbook of Religious Epistemology*. Cambridge: Cambridge University Press, 13–28.

Baker-Hytch, M., & Benton, M. A. (2015). Defeatism Defeated. *Philosophical Perspectives*, **29**(1), 40–66.

Benton, M. A. (2017). Epistemology Personalized. *The Philosophical Quarterly*, **67**(269), 813–34.

Benton, M. A., Hawthorne, J., & Isaacs, Y. (2016). Evil and Evidence. *Oxford Studies in Philosophy of Religion*, **7**, 1–31.

Bergmann, M. (1997). Internalism, Externalism and the No-Defeater Condition. *Synthese*, **110**(3), 399–417.

(2021). *Radical Skepticism and Epistemic Intuition*. Oxford: Oxford University Press.

Boghossian, P. (2001). Inference and Insight. *Philosophy and Phenomenological Research*, **63**(3), 633–40.

Braddock, M. (2023). Natural Nonbelief in God: Prehistoric Humans, Divine Hiddenness, and Debunking. In D. E. Machuca, ed., *Evolutionary Debunking Arguments: Ethics, Philosophy of Religion, Philosophy of Mathematics, Metaphysics, and Epistemology*. New York, NY: Routledge, 160–84.

Carr, B. (2008). Cosmology and Religion. In P. Clayton, ed., *The Oxford Handbook of Religion and Science*. Oxford: Oxford University Press, 139–55.

Clark, A., & Chalmers, D. J. (1998). The Extended Mind. *Analysis*, **58**(1), 7–19.

Clark, K. J., & Barrett, J. L. (2011). Reidian Religious Epistemology and the Cognitive Science of Religion. *Journal of the American Academy of Religion*, **79**(2), 1–37.

Collins, D. (2022). *The Hunt for the Silver Killer*. London: Simon & Schuster.

Cottingham, J. (2005). *The Spiritual Dimension: Religion, Philosophy, and Value*. Cambridge: Cambridge University Press.

Craig, W. L., & Moreland, J. P. (2009). Introduction. In W. L. Craig & J. P. Moreland, eds., *The Blackwell Companion to Natural Theology*. Oxford: Blackwell, ix–xiii.

Dalal, N. (2021). Advaita Vedānta. In S. Goetz & C. Taliaferro, eds., *The Encyclopedia of Philosophy of Religion*. London: John Wiley & Sons.

Dennett, D. (2007). You Have to Give up Your Intuitions about Consciousness. In S. Blackmore, ed., *Conversations on Consciousness: What the Best Minds Think about the Brain, Free Will, and What It Means to Be Human*. Oxford: Oxford University Press, 79–91.

Descartes, R. (1988 [1641]). Meditations on First Philosophy. In J. Cottingham, R. Stoothoff, & D. Murdoch, eds., *The Philosophical Writings of Descartes*. Cambridge: Cambridge University Press.

Draper, P. (2002). Seeing but Not Believing: Confessions of a Practicing Agnostic. In D. Howard-Snyder & P. K. Moser, eds., *Divine Hiddenness: New Essays*. Cambridge: Cambridge University Press, 197–214.

(2010). Cumulative Cases. In C. Taliaferro, P. Draper, & P. L. Quinn, eds., *A Companion to Philosophy of Religion*. Malden, MA: Blackwell, 414–24.

Fitelson, B. (2001). A Bayesian Account of Independent Evidence with Applications. *Philosophy of Science*, **68**(3), S123–S140.

(2007). Likelihoodism, Bayesianism, and Relational Confirmation. *Synthese*, **156**(3), 473–89.

Goldberg, S. (2014). Does Externalist Epistemology Rationalize Religious Commitment? In L. F. Callahan & T. O'Connor, eds., *Religious Faith and Intellectual Virtue*. Oxford: Oxford University Press, 279–98.

Goldie, P. (2000). *The Emotions: A Philosophical Exploration*. Oxford: Oxford University Press.

Hawthorne, J. 2013. Theism, Atheism, and Bayesianism: Part 1. *Philosophy of Cosmology Conference 'Is "God" Explanatory?'*. St Anne's College, Oxford. www.youtube.com/watch?v=ItV-gPtxtL0.

Hepburn, R. W. (1963). From World to God. *Mind*, **72**(285), 40–50.

Hick, J. (1979). *Evil and the God of Love*. Glasgow: Collins.

(1989). *An Interpretation of Religion: Human Responses to the Transcendent*. New Haven, CT: Yale University Press.

Hirsch, S. R. (1960 [1836]). *The Nineteen Letters about Judaism*. New York, NY: Philip Feldheim.

Howard-Snyder, D., & Moser, P. K., eds. (2002). *Divine Hiddenness: New Essays*. Cambridge: Cambridge University Press.

Jackson, F. (1986). What Mary Didn't Know. *The Journal of Philosophy*, **83**(5), 291–5.

James, W. (1979 [1896]). *The Will to Believe and Other Essays in Popular Philosophy*. Cambridge, MA: Harvard University Press.

Kelly, T. (2014). Evidence. *Stanford Encyclopedia of Philosophy*. https://plato .stanford.edu/archives/win2016/entries/evidence.

Kopec, M., & Titelbaum, M. G. (2016). The Uniqueness Thesis. *Philosophy Compass*, **11**(4), 189–200.

Kvanvig, J. L. (2002). Divine Hiddenness: What Is the Problem? In D. Howard-Snyder & P. K. Moser, eds., *Divine Hiddenness: New Essays*. Cambridge: Cambridge University Press, 149–63.

Lasonen-Aarnio, M. (2014). Higher-Order Evidence and the Limits of Defeat. *Philosophy and Phenomenological Research*, **88**(2), 314–45.

Lebens, S. (2022). Defining Religion. *Oxford Studies in Philosophy of Religion*, **10**, 145–68.

Leftow, B. (2016). Naturalistic Pantheism. In A. Buckareff & Y. Nagasawa, eds., *Alternative Concepts of God: Essays on the Metaphysics of the Divine*. Oxford: Oxford University Press, 64–88.

Leslie, J. (2016). A Way of Picturing God. In A. Buckareff & Y. Nagasawa, eds., *Alternative Concepts of God: Essays on the Metaphysics of the Divine*. Oxford: Oxford University Press, 50–63.

Maitzen, S. (2006). Divine Hiddenness and the Demographics of Theism. *Religious Studies*, **42**(2), 177–91.

Marsh, J. (2013). Darwin and the Problem of Natural Nonbelief. *The Monist*, **96**(3), 349–76.

   (2017). On the Socratic Injunction to Follow the Argument Where It Leads. In P. Draper & J. L. Schellenberg, eds., *Renewing Philosophy of Religion: Exploratory Essays*. Oxford: Oxford University Press, 187–207.

Mawson, T. J. (2013). The Case against Atheism. In S. Bullivant & M. Ruse, eds., *The Oxford Handbook of Atheism*. Oxford: Oxford University Press, 22–36.

McCauley, R. (2011). *Why Religion Is Natural and Science Is Not*. New York, NY: Oxford University Press.

McGrew, T. & Depoe, J. M. (2013). Natural Theology and the Uses of Argument. *Philosophia Christi*, **15**(2), 299–309.

McKim, R. (2001). *Religious Ambiguity and Religious Diversity.* Oxford: Oxford University Press.

Mitchell, B. (1973). *The Justification of Religious Belief.* London: Macmillan.

Moore, G. E. (1962). *Philosophical Papers.* New York, NY: Collier Books.

Moser, P. K. (2004). Divine Hiddenness Does Not Justify Atheism. In M. L. Peterson & R. J. Van Arragon, eds., *Contemporary Debates in the Philosophy of Religion.* Oxford: Blackwell, 42–54.

(2010). *The Evidence for God: Religious Knowledge Reexamined.* Cambridge: Cambridge University Press.

Newman, J. H. (1872). *Fifteen Sermons Preached before the University of Oxford.* London: Longmans, Green and Co

Nozick, R. (1989). *The Examined Life: Philosophical Meditations.* New York, NY: Simon & Schuster.

Nussbaum, M. (1990). *Love's Knowledge.* Oxford: Oxford University Press.

Oppy, G. (2006). *Arguing about Gods.* Cambridge: Cambridge University Press.

(2017). Rationality and Worldview. In P. Draper & J. L. Schellenberg, eds., *Renewing Philosophy of Religion: Exploratory Essays.* Oxford: Oxford University Press, 174–86.

Page, B. (2020). Arguing to Theism from Consciousness. *Faith and Philosophy*, **37**(3), 336–62.

Parsons, K. M. (2013). Perspectives on Natural Theology from Analytic Philosophy. In R. Re Manning, J. Hedley Brooke, & F. Watts, eds., *The Oxford Handbook of Natural Theology.* Oxford: Oxford University Press, 248–61.

Pascal, B. (1995 [1669]). *Pensées.* London: Penguin Classics.

Penelhum, T. (1971). *Religion and Rationality: An Introduction to the Philosophy of Religion.* New York, NY: Random House.

Pittard, J. (2020). *Disagreement, Deference, and Religious Commitment.* Oxford: Oxford University Press.

Plantinga, A. (1974). *The Nature of Necessity.* Oxford: Clarendon Press.

(2000). *Warranted Christian Belief.* Oxford: Oxford University Press.

Pollock, J. L. (1986). *Contemporary Theories of Knowledge.* Totowa, NJ: Rowman & Littlefield.

Poston, T. (2018). The Argument from (A) to (Y): The Argument from So Many Arguments. In J. L. Walls & T. Dougherty, eds., *Two Dozen (or So) Arguments for God.* Oxford: Oxford University Press, 372–88.

Pritchard, D. (2005). *Epistemic Luck.* Oxford: Oxford University Press.

(2010). Cognitive Ability and the Extended Cognition Thesis. *Synthese*, **175**(1), 133–51.

Quine, W. V. O. (1953). *From a Logical Point of View*. Cambridge, MA: Harvard University Press.

Rowe, W. L. (1979). The Problem of Evil and Some Varieties of Atheism. *American Philosophical Quarterly*, **16**(4), 335–41.

Royall, R. (1997). *Statistical Evidence: A Likelihood Paradigm*. London: Chapman and Hill.

Salvi, C., Bricolo, E., Kounios, J., Bowden, E., & Beeman, M. (2016). Insight Solutions Are Correct More Often Than Analytic Solutions. *Thinking & Reasoning*, **22**(4), 443–60.

Schellenberg, J. L. (1993). *Divine Hiddenness and Human Reason*. Ithaca, NY: Cornell University Press.

(2007). *The Wisdom to Doubt: A Justification of Religious Skepticism*. Ithaca, NY: Cornell University Press.

(2015). *The Hiddenness Argument*. Oxford: Oxford University Press.

(2016). God for All Time: From Theism to Ultimism. In A. Buckareff & Y. Nagasawa, eds., *Alternative Concepts of God: Essays on the Metaphysics of the Divine*. Oxford: Oxford University Press, 164–77.

Stump, E. (2010). *Wandering in Darkness*. Oxford: Oxford University Press.

Stump, E. & Green, A., eds. (2015). *Hidden Divinity and Religious Belief: New Perspectives*. Cambridge: Cambridge University Press.

Swinburne, R. (1998). *Providence and the Problem of Evil*. Oxford: Oxford University Press.

(2004). *The Existence of God*, 2nd ed. Oxford: Oxford University Press.

Tucker, C., ed. (2013). *Seemings and Justification: New Essays on Dogmatism and Phenomenal Conservatism*. Oxford: Oxford University Press.

Vainio, O.-P. (2018). *Cosmology in Theological Perspective: Understanding Our Place in the Universe*. Grand Rapids, MI: Baker Academic.

Weidner, V. (2021). *Divine Hiddenness*. Cambridge: Cambridge University Press.

White, R. (2005). Epistemic Permissiveness. *Philosophical Perspectives*, **19**(1), 445–59.

Williamson, T. (2000). *Knowledge and Its Limits*. Oxford: Oxford University Press.

Wynn, M. (1999). *God and Goodness: A Natural Theological Perspective*. London: Routledge.

(2005). *Emotional Experience and Religious Understanding: Integrating Perception, Conception and Feeling*. Cambridge: Cambridge University Press.

(2009). *Faith and Place: An Essay in Embodied Epistemology*. Oxford: Oxford University Press.

(2020). *Spiritual Traditions and the Virtues: Living between Heaven and Earth*. Oxford: Oxford University Press.

Acknowledgements

I am very grateful for comments and discussion on earlier drafts of this Element to Miles Donahue, Charity Anderson, Matthew Benton, Mark Wynn, Alanzo Paul, and Michael Bergmann. I also benefitted from the feedback that I received from two anonymous reviewers for Cambridge University Press.

Cambridge Elements ☰

The Problems of God

Series Editor

Michael L. Peterson
Asbury Theological Seminary

Michael L. Peterson is Professor of Philosophy at Asbury Theological Seminary. He is the author of *God and Evil* (Routledge); *Monotheism, Suffering, and Evil* (Cambridge University Press); *With All Your Mind* (University of Notre Dame Press); *C. S. Lewis and the Christian Worldview* (Oxford University Press); *Evil and the Christian God* (Baker Book House); and *Philosophy of Education: Issues and Options* (Intervarsity Press). He is co-author of *Reason and Religious Belief* (Oxford University Press); *Science, Evolution, and Religion: A Debate about Atheism and Theism* (Oxford University Press); and *Biology, Religion, and Philosophy* (Cambridge University Press). He is editor of *The Problem of Evil: Selected Readings* (University of Notre Dame Press). He is co-editor of *Philosophy of Religion: Selected Readings* (Oxford University Press) and *Contemporary Debates in Philosophy of Religion* (Wiley-Blackwell). He served as General Editor of the Blackwell monograph series Exploring Philosophy of Religion and is founding Managing Editor of the journal *Faith and Philosophy.*

About the Series

This series explores problems related to God, such as the human quest for God or gods, contemplation of God, and critique and rejection of God. Concise, authoritative volumes in this series will reflect the methods of a variety of disciplines, including philosophy of religion, theology, religious studies, and sociology.

Cambridge Elements ☰

The Problems of God

Elements in the Series

Divine Guidance: Moral Attraction in Action
Paul K. Moser

God, Salvation, and the Problem of Spacetime
Emily Qureshi-Hurst

Orthodoxy and Heresy
Steven Nemes

God and Political Theory
Tyler Dalton McNabb

Evolution and Christianity
Michael Ruse

Evil and Theodicy
Laura W. Ekstrom

A full series listing is available at: www.cambridge.org/EPOG

Printed in the United States
by Baker & Taylor Publisher Services